HENRY JAMES, SR.
AND THE RELIGION OF COMMUNITY

HENRY JAMES, SR. AND THE RELIGION OF COMMUNITY

By

DWIGHT W. HOOVER

WILLIAM B. EERDMANS PUBLISHING COMPANY
GRAND RAPIDS, MICHIGAN

Preface

The purpose of this book is to portray the religious thought of the elder Henry James in terms of its nineteenth-century setting. The work is not designed to be biographical; the biographical material that is included is intended to shed light on different aspects of James's thought. Nor is it the author's purpose to trace the influence of James upon his two more famous sons. James's ideas, it seems to me, are important enough to stand on their own merits.

In our own times the ideas of Henry James have uses. Attempts by theologians like Harvey Cox (*The Secular City*) to de-institutionalize the church and to make religion integral with city life are foreshadowed by James. In a period when religious movements were becoming institutionalized in the United States — Methodism, Christian Science, Christian Education — James proclaimed a sweeping anti-institutionalism and secularization in terms that are surprisingly contemporary.

In addition, James had views of man and his environment conflicting with the romantic assumptions of the nineteenth century. In an age that idealized nature and solitary pursuits, James insisted that nature reflected man, not vice versa, and that society was better than solitude. To leave a utopian Garden of Eden was to step up the ladder of progress. The anti-city bias evident in many of James's contemporaries is missing in James; he welcomed the coming of the city even if this coming brought sin and evil. Institutions had an educative purpose, and the city was an excellent school.

This is not to argue that James was a twentieth-century radical theologian or city booster. It is to say that to neglect the thought of James is to neglect a source of ordered ideas which are, in some ways, contrary to our common assumptions about the nineteenth century. Certainly James was a product of his time, but that time was more rich and complex than we realize or than our categories encompass. Surely there is room for another James in our galaxy of nineteenth-century social thinkers.

5

It goes without saying that the ideas contained herein are derived from many sources, from the community, as James would say. My intellectual debts far outstrip my capital, but I received major help from Stow Persons, who called my attention to Henry James, Sr., and provided a structure of knowledge in which he could be placed. The errors in the study are, of course, my own.

Then too, I owe much to my wife, who has more faith in me than I have in myself.

Contents

	Preface	5
	Introduction	9
1	On Backgrounds	13
2	Orthodox Swedenborgianism	32
3	Basic Religious Premises	43
4	Nature of Man	74
5	Society and Institutions	98
6	Consequences	124
	Conclusion	138
	Bibliography	141
	Index	149

Introduction

The period of time covered by the written work of Henry James, Sr., approximates thirty-nine years, from the publication of Remarks on the *Apostolic Gospel* in 1840 to *Society the Redeemed Form of Man* in 1879. This period saw perhaps more changes in modes of life and thought than any other in American history; out of these changes grew a new society.

Politically, this was the period of the death of one major party, the Whigs, and the growth of a third party, the Republicans, to the position of dominance that had been vacated. The problems which, by their very nature, effectively wrought the political upheaval were slavery, states rights, territorial expansion and organization, war, and the reconstruction following this cataclysmic event. The transition from political control exercised by a party pledged to support agricultural and laboring interests to control by a party dedicated to the furtherance of industrial growth was accomplished with maximum speed, although the society produced by these political attitudes differed greatly.

Social change proceeded rapidly; crusades were the order of the day. Voluntary movements sprang up to sanctify men and make them free through religion and education. For men who were already free, voluntary associations existed to help these men achieve perfection.[1] Reform groups ranged from those trying to free the slaves to those campaigning for an improved diet. No part of society was untouched or unaffected. Only the coming of the Civil War blighted the bright hopes of these pilgrims, and only the march of postwar society toward the fussy gingerbread of the "Gilded Age" caused them to be forgotten.

The 1840's "were the days of the march of the intellect. . . . Education was the word in Boston, as a generation later the word was culture."[2] But the belief in the efficacy of reason which characterized the American Enlightenment was tempered by a

---

[1] Gilbert Seldes, *The Stammering Century* (New York: John Day, 1927), p. 6.

[2] Van Wyck Brooks, *The Flowering of New England* (New York: E. P. Dutton, Inc., 1940), p. 172.

new interest in religion, which provided a foundation for the humanitarian movements of the day. Maintaining a judicious balance between an emotional religious appeal and a rational intellectual one proved difficult. By 1850 the compromise was breaking, just as the Missouri Compromise was failing on the political level; and the emotional element seemed to be gaining ascendency.[3] The 1860's were martial years, concerned with the social displacement of an internecine war and subsequent peace, while the 1870's and the corruption of Grant's administrations hailed the beginnings of the "gospel of Wealth" with material goals predominant.

Political and social changes supplemented each other in this forty-year span. The trends in social and political life, which became all too evident after Appomattox, had their roots in pre-war society.[4] Older societal and political ties had been in the process of change for some time, the former by the systematic elimination of the Puritan ethos, retained though weakened by enlightened social theory, and the latter through the gradual emergence of political parties out of the remains of old factions and the hardening of factional disputes into party platforms.

The problem confronting American society was no less than the formation of a new society and a new state. Man had a unique opportunity to mold the world into a satisfying shape.

> The only limits to the diversity of new faiths in the first half of the nineteenth century were the limits of men's own differences and of their aspirations and imaginations. . . . Every aspect of society and every phase of life were subject to the eager scrutiny of inquiring minds, and the optimistic liberalism of the day caused men to believe in the possibility of creating a new heaven and a new earth by the intensity of their efforts and the efficacy of their faith.[5]

This ideal motivated many of the intellectual expressions of the period. Emerson, Thoreau, Hawthorne, Melville, and Whitman critically evaluated individuals and institutions, hoping to determine the faith of the former which had produced the latter. Out of this critical summation might come a new society, superior to the old, combining the best elements of the past with the best

---

[3] F. L. Pattee, *The Feminine Fifties* (New York: D. Appleton-Century, 1940), pp. 9-10.

[4] Lewis Mumford, *The Golden Age* (New York: Boni and Liveright, 1926), pp. 86-87.

[5] Alice Felt Tyler, *Freedom's Ferment* (Minneapolis: University of Minnesota, 1944), p. 46.

theoretical designs for the future.[6] The main question by which institutions and ideas were measured was: What was the guiding idea or genius of America and how could that spirit be best expressed in institutional forms? The question was infinitely complex. Its counterpart on the practical level was the task of unifying the political and social life of America around universal American forms. Both the practical and theoretical answers to this question of the American spirit and its institutional embodiment, as these answers emerged from the Civil War, proved disquieting and unsatisfying. Which had failed, the ideals or the practical attempt to achieve these ideals? The problem of American life remained unsolved.

The essence of James's period is exceedingly difficult to grasp since this was a time of rapid change. Political and social changes are in themselves difficult to understand in periods of enormous flux, for the old merges with the new incompletely, leaving vestiges of the old which the new has not replaced. Even more difficult to grasp are the changes wrought by new methods of thinking, as in this case the elements of intuitional transcendentalism mingled with evolutionary naturalism.

Henry James participated in the questioning of the society in which he found himself. The forces of that society pressed upon him as they pressed upon his contemporaries. The problem of evaluating the past, especially as it affected the prediction of the future, concerned him. But his views on the questions of the day proved unacceptable to his contemporaries, largely because these views were couched in a traditional theological language, which was losing favor. James's opinions exhibited some of the thought of his day, although the changes in this thought over a period of time did not visibly shake his intellectual framework.

James believed in the perfectibility of both man and society, and he therefore attempted to compromise between the perfectionism of his time which led to radical individualism and anti-institutionalism, and the perfectionism which led to a utopian socialism and the postulation of perfect institutions. While believing in the social nature of salvation, James did not believe in the attempt at collectivism in his own time. Like Leo Marx, James tried in religion to achieve a middle landscape where the best of two possible worlds could be had.

---

[6] Mumford, p. 92.

One

On Backgrounds

James's thought concerned itself with traditional religious problems and was expressed in religious terms. Although most of his contemporaries could understand James, they found his vocabulary and his views unacceptable. They were concerned with different problems and new definitions. It is the purpose of this chapter to trace the religious tradition leading to James; to indicate what certain terms meant to the Calvinist, the Unitarian, and the Transcendentalist; to set up a background against which James may be placed. James's ideas came from many sources, including these historic American religious movements, particularly Calvinism, and were sharpened against the hard stones of the Unitarian and Transcendental theology of his time. In order to understand James best the views of these three groups must be briefly mentioned.

The original religious influence in the American colonies had been predominantly Protestant, with Calvinism being the strongest Protestant element. Dominating as it did the religious arena, Calvinism provided the main ideological basis for the social, economic and political thought of the colonies. Within Calvinistic theories, however, there were conflicts which were disguised with varying degrees of success. The most difficult compromise was to reconcile the necessarily individual experience of conversion with the social nature of church discipline upon which society and government were based. How was it possible to maintain a high level of competence in society and government if the composition of these institutions was determined by individual conviction? Since a man had to be a church member to participate actively in society and government, might not any man fake conversion in order to gain this power? Calvinists had an all too vivid picture of what might happen if the discipline of the church were lightened in

favor of individual freedom; the excesses of antinomian enthusi-
asm had provided that. The path favored by American Calvinists
was that fraught with the least danger, that is, to prefer Christian order to Christian liberty. Some Calvinists of the colonial era
objected to this compromise and it was equally distasteful to nineteenth-century thinkers with their passion for liberty. Nonetheless,
Calvinist religious thought reached a peak of sophistication from
which it was removed with difficulty.

Emphasizing God primarily, the Calvinist only secondarily considered society, man's relation with man. The concept of God
was the core of religious theory. For the Calvinists, God was love,
love capable of being expressed only to being, both finite and infinite, man and God. Since infinite being was superior to finite
being, love shown to man was less important than that shown
by God to the qualities of His perfection. If the two loves con-
flicted, the highest good was to prevail. God's justice and power
ought to be displayed in man and the universe. "If the misery of
a sinner is conducive to such a display, which it must be because
sinners are in fact miserable, then it is just and good that sinners
should be punished with misery."[1] Man ought, in the classical
Calvinist example, to be willing to be damned for the greater glory
of God, since the misery of man was unimportant when compared
with the higher good of God's glory.

This was hard doctrine, suitable only to tough minds; but it
was rational, proceeding from the original premise of God's nature.
Man's nature, Puritan theory held, displayed a duality, one part
gross and evil with a concern for the flesh, the other good with a
concern for the spirit. Whether man's nature motivated him to
good or evil, God was responsible since He had so created man.
The individual, then, was incapable of true virtue or vice.[2] Perhaps
an idea like this was too heretical for Calvinists to accept. At any
rate, early in the colonial period Calvinists started to modify the
position of God and man by insisting that man had a certain
responsibility for the evil he did. A typical statement of this is
the following, made by a doctrinally acceptable Calvinist minister:
"Sin and guilt (so far as I can see) are personal as much as knowledge."[3] Now if man's sin was regarded as his own responsibility
and not as God's, a long step towards the destruction of Puritan
piety had been taken, for that piety assumed that the most radical

---

[1] Joseph Haroutunian, *Pietism versus Moralism* (New York: Henry Holt,
1932), p. 144.
[2] *Ibid.*, p. 227.

error possible was the notion that salvation was attainable through human effort. And if sin were personal, might not salvation as well be personal and attainable through human effort?

Many elements of the Bible had been incorporated into Calvinist doctrine, including the belief that the new dispensation given by Christ had substituted baptism for the Hebrew custom of circumcision.[4] The Hebraic emphasis upon morality, however, had been amended in Calvinism. Moral action was a product of personal effort and was not to be confused with Christian piety, as morality was a part of the natural world while piety was part of a supernatural one. Man might act as a saint yet not possess a sense of dependence upon God, and only God determined man's salvation or damnation.

But a distinction between a morally good man and a pious man was not one which man could make, and yet the church was composed, supposedly, of men chosen by God. For a short time, people of considerable personal merit exerted pressure to be admitted to the functions of the state through church membership. On the one hand, some evidence of God's favor must be admitted to maintain a church; on the other hand, there must always be an insistence upon the omnipotence of God and the insufficiency of man's effort in achieving salvation. This was a precarious balance, capable of causing no end of difficulty.

The opening wedges to affirm man's power at God's expense were furnished by the attribution of personal sin to man and by using good conduct as a partial test for church membership. Ministers like Samuel Hopkins, intent upon attracting prospective converts through humanizing dogma, helped accomplish a higher estimation of man by reconsidering the nature of sin. Earlier, sin had been contrasted to good and had provided examples of the glory of God, but now Hopkins said that God allowed sin "because through divine intervention it is conducive to the good of the universe, and not because it is a manifestation of the glory of God."[5] The implicit assumption here seemed to be that the good of the universe was the good of God.

A concern with the universe might cause God to concentrate His love upon man, the most important being in the universe. Gradually, the Calvinists were coming to this position. Assuming that the universe was more important to God than anything else, man could help God by improving the universe. If the primary

[3] *Ibid.*
[4] *Ibid.*, p. 106.
[5] *Ibid.*, pp. 39-40.

goal of God was the creation of a moral universe, as later Calvinists came to believe,[6] then man had a much more important role in the universe than earlier thinkers had conceded.

Support for the modifications of Puritan thought came from people who disliked the restrictive elements in it and denied its validity in the social and political realm. "Owen with his 'counter-acting circumstances' and the phrenologists with their 'faculties' were as effectively hostile as the infidels who denied the story of Adam's fall, and the Universalists who taught that all men are saved. . . ."[7] Perhaps these similar attacks were all symptomatic of the lost value of Puritanism. The society based upon the elect had become secularized, so that enlightened social thought posited a society ideally based upon the visible results of virtue and genius, both partially derivative from human effort. The newer organizations of society and government had bypassed Puritan theory, although some elements of that theory lingered for a considerable length of time, indicating that the utility of any ideology can be an index of its acceptance and popularity.

Here we reach the end of the modification of Calvinist thought within its own framework and turn to some institutional offshoots. A major change in religious thought was shown by the transition from Calvinism to Unitarianism. Congregation after congregation in New England turned from a concept of a triune God to a unitary one. This change proceeded during the latter part of the eighteenth century and the earlier part of the nineteenth. The Buckminister family presents a typical example of the changing nature of New England churches. Reverend Joseph Buckminister, a "stern old Calvinist," preached strictly Calvinistic doctrinal sermons, while his son, Reverend Joseph Steven, preached less on doctrine and more on practical living, together with a sprinkling of Biblical criticism.[8]

As this example might indicate, the difference between the "New England theology" and the Unitarian position consisted largely of matters of emphasis. God remained omnipotent and just for the Unitarians, although His intelligence and love were mentioned more often. The Scriptures were accepted as sufficient and as divinely inspired, and miracles were retained to support Christian revelation. The Unitarians, however, viewed miracles as con-

---

[6] *Ibid.,* p. 87.

[7] Gilbert Seldes, *The Stammering Century,* pp. 359-360.

[8] Harold Clarke Goddard, *Studies in New England Transcendentalism* (New York: Columbia University, 1908), p. 27.

firming the faith men had in revelation rather than forming the basis for this faith. The acceptance of miracles served to separate Unitarians from natural religionists who rejected miracles.[9]

Channing, the outstanding if atypical spokesman for the Unitarians of the 1820's, condensed his religious ideas into three: "the loving kindness of God," "the nobility of man," and "the joy of a religious life."[10] These were not in any order of importance, however much critics might allege that the second outweighed the first. Channing's view of man was, however, more optimistic than that of other Unitarians.

God was love to Channing, just as He had been to the Calvinists. However, this love took for Channing a different form. God's love was measured by His goodness, and this goodness was revealed to man through creation.[11] Hopkins had viewed the love of God from only a slightly different angle in his Calvinist theology. The visible evidence in nature of God's love was not a strikingly original thought, but it was extremely important in Channing's thought in tying man to God. The love God showed to man enabled man to come into a closer union with Him. One notes that God had to prove His love for man; man no longer accepted this love as an article of faith.

Besides possessing an overwhelming love for man, God had a sense of rightness never to be shaken. As Channing said: "We believe that in no being is the sense of right so strange, so omnipotent, as in God. We believe that His almighty power is entirely submitted to His perceptions of rectitude; and this is the ground of our piety."[12] God was not entirely omnipotent, being bound Himself to follow His own concept of a moral law. One could conclude from this, as later Unitarians sometimes did, that God differed only in degree from man, having been perfected and purified. If few Unitarians of Channing's day would go this far, more would agree, however, that the ways of Channing's God were more scrutable to man than the Calvinist had allowed, for God had always to act in a moral fashion.

Another attribute of God was mercy, which, like power, was conditioned upon the interests of virtue. Forgiving sins was not a blind, instinctive act on God's part; rather He would make the

---

[9] Stow Persons, *Free Religion* (New Haven: Yale University, 1947), p. 4.

[10] Alice Felt Tyler, *Freedom's Ferment*, p. 27.

[11] William Ellery Channing, *Works* (Boston: American Unitarian Association, 1899), p. 317.

[12] *Ibid.*, p. 376.

granting of mercy compatible with the demands of morality.[13] If God was not all-powerful, neither was He all-merciful.

Given the expression of God's mercy and power along moral lines, Channing found it much simpler to predict God. Man became more capable of understanding God and of conforming to God's will. This meant more freedom for man, an essential tenet for the early Unitarians. Mayhew, one of the earliest of Unitarians, assumed that the freedom of man was more certain than the truth of Christianity.[14] Liberty was the highest good in man, traceable back to Christ who gave it. From religious liberty came secular liberties, civil and political, to grace men's institutions.[15] Freedom meant nobility since only freedom gave men the power to make moral judgments, to abjure low passions which previously intrigued him, and to choose higher ones.[16] The inability of man to shape his own destiny gave rise to the belief that man could approximate God's will through his own efforts.[17]

Puritan thought had denied the ability of man to achieve any good under his own power, but an opening was left for the power of God's grace to change the world. Grace was the single, important instrument bringing about regeneration and salvation, for only by this contribution of God's power could man achieve the good. What room, then, had the Unitarians left for grace? Unitarians retained the belief in grace as a means of salvation but placed grace under the subjection of love and righteousness, denying its arbitrary exercise.[18] Of course, the emphasis upon man's ability diminished the importance of grace as a free gift.

If man was created free and was capable of understanding God's will to some degree, he must be endowed by God with reason. Given this instrument, the temptation to turn it upon traditional religious dogmas proved too great to resist. The doctrines of the trinity,[19] original depravity,[20] and outward hell[21] could not stand the cold, hard light of reason and so were either discarded or changed. The most famous of these, the doctrine of the trinity, was altered so that Christ was said to be united

---

13 *Ibid.*

14 George Willis Cooke, *Unitarianism in America* (Boston: American Unitarian Association, 1910), p. 62.

15 Channing, *Works,* p. 172.

16 *Ibid.,* p. 174.

17 Haroutunian, p. 208.

18 Cooke, p. 62.

19 Channing, *Works,* p. 244.

20 *Ibid.,* p. 245.

21 *Ibid.,* p. 252.

with God intimately, and not personally, thus substituting the ambiguous for the specific.[22]

Most historic religious thought accepted the validity of reason as a tool in helping man to achieve a truer knowledge of God but denied that reason could challenge tradition. Compromise between the two, reason and tradition, marked most religious thinking. If the Unitarians would pursue reason as far as it led, they might find themselves near the position of natural religion, in which reason destroyed revelation. This the Unitarians refused to do. Channing denied that any conflict existed between reason and revelation, since these instruments for truth supported each other.[23] He admitted, however, that revelation was far more probable and suitable in ancient Biblical settings because God then instructed men directly,[24] while modern society was less in need of revelation since reason had been more fully evolved and was more successful. Revelation remained historically important primarily as the origin of men's knowledge.

Reason did not contradict revelation; neither did it contradict miracles. The universe was not a machine from which God had absented Himself; nor was the universe good in itself. Developed by God for its use to man, the universe instructed man by variation in its natural order, sacrificing internal consistency for this more important purpose.[25] Miracles were an exception to the norm of order in the universe; God was not immanent in the world of nature but entered into it on occasions. This view of nature did not differ greatly from the Puritan one. Transcendentalists, however, criticized the cosmology, taking exception to miracles and to a semi-mechanical view of the world.

One would suppose that, given all the universe to instruct him through his reason, man would not err. Yet the Unitarians held that he fell short of the ideal. What constituted sin for the Unitarians? To sin was to outrage one's own sense of right and wrong by thinking and acting in willfully wrong ways; to fail to give God the obedience, thanks, and reverence which one feels He should have; to break the moral law regulating one's relation with his neighbors.[26] This definition of sin differs greatly from that of original Puritan thought. Little mention is made of man's disbelief or lack of faith in God. Since God was not a distant deity

---

[22] Haroutunian, p. 195.
[23] Channing, *Works,* p. 239.
[24] *Ibid.,* p. 193.
[25] *Ibid.,* p. 211.
[26] *Ibid.,* p. 347.

demanding justice but rather was a part of man's inner nature, man sinned in not fulfilling the best in himself. Calvinism maintained that man was sinful in himself; for even if man lived up to the highest promise in himself, he would still be sinful. The Unitarians held out the hope of permanent improvement through personal means instead.

The Unitarian concept of sin is seen best in the light of the agent that reveals this sin. Sin was discovered by reason, conscience, and the moral faculty, all of which could be unified into a single concept.[27] God did not reveal sin to man except as He gave man reason to discover sin; it was man's obligation to ferret out sin for himself. Assumptions like this reveal part of the Unitarian view on the nature of man. Man contains the element of perfection within him; he sins when he deviates from this inner ideal that he possesses.[28]

If reason is equated with the moral faculty, as Unitarians held, it follows logically that as man becomes more reasonable he also becomes capable of more sophisticated moral decisions. Assuming that only man could improve his moral faculty, Channing believed that freedom to develop was essential for the growth of morality. God could not make man virtuous even in heaven; man must do that for himself or risk violating the sense of morality present in God and himself. Concentrating more and more upon morality, the Unitarians demoted piety to an imitation of God on this earth combined with a sense of moderate dependence upon God.[29] Moralism had almost completely triumphed over piety; an emphasis upon the glory of God had been replaced by an emphasis upon the nobility of man.

If God Himself was unable to give man virtue, could society hope to do so? Channing was inclined to say no, since he suspected society of preventing individual moral judgments.[30] Accepting the premise that moral judgments were the chief characteristic of a spiritual man made societal perversion extremely dangerous. Society could and should function as a stimulus to man's activity but it should never dull his sense of morality.

Given this duty of society, the great benefit of free institutions came from their ability to offer superior stimulus with few restrictions on moral judgments. Government had two functions. The negative function was to prevent people from destroying one

---

27 *Ibid.*, p. 15.
28 *Ibid.*, p. 292.
29 *Ibid.*, p. 386.
30 *Ibid.*, p. 144.

another. The positive function was the education of men. Participation in government, local or national, taught men to live together, thus enhancing their moral sense. The freer the institution was, the greater the moral improvement.

A poor institution could be distinguished by the lack of education it gave men in social action. No good society could tolerate an organized priesthood, for the essence of society required that sanctity be a property of all classes, rather than of a single one.[31] Every man was to possess the sacerdotal function, just as every Calvinist was a combination priest and king. The best society was, therefore, the one in which each individual participated fully in the organized functions of the church and state.

From the Calvinist idea of the glory of God had evolved the idea of the freedom and nobility of man. This came about through a gradual reappraisal of doctrines, which were then discounted and discarded, retained and amended, or elevated and emphasized. God was made more human as man was made more God-like. Piety and morality had merged.

Unitarianism with its combination of new ideas and old proved unsatisfactory for many nineteenth-century people. Romantic elements were filtering into American thought, reacting against the seemingly excessive rationalism of the eighteenth century. Unitarianism was regarded by man as an offspring of this rationalism and was therefore unacceptable. The situation at this time was aptly summed up by Orestes Brownson in *The Convert,* his autobiography, written in later years after he had become a Catholic convert.

> Men are beginning to understand that Protestantism is no-churchism, is no positive religion; and while it serves the purpose of criticism and destruction, it cannot meet the wants of the soul, or erect the temple in which the human race may assemble to worship in concord and peace. Unitarianism has demolished Calvinism, made an end in all thinking minds of everything like dogmatic Protestantism, and Unitarianism itself satisfies nobody. It is negative, cold, lifeless, and all advanced minds among Unitarianism are dissatisfied with it, and are craving something higher, better, more living, and lifegiving. ... Society as it is, is a lie, a sham, a charnel-house, a valley of dry bones. ... So I felt and so felt others; and whoever enjoyed the confidence of the leading Unitarian ministers in Boston and its vicinity from 1830 to 1840, well knows that they were sick at heart with what they would find shelter from the

---

[31] *Ibid.,* p. 209.

storms of this wintry world, and some crumbs of the bread of life to keep them from starving.[32]

Like the Unitarians, most Transcendentalists came from Calvinist roots. Like Channing, Emerson turned from Calvinism because he was revolted by the doctrine of total depravity and had encountered Quakerism and the mysticism of Swedenborg.[33] A. Bronson Alcott had experienced the same formative influences except that his background was Episcopalian rather than Calvinist.[34] Theodore Parker's family were Congregationalists of orthodox Puritan bent; and Margaret Fuller also had Puritan roots.[35]

By no means all of the Unitarians were impressed with the new Transcendental ideas. Indeed, the opposition to these ideas was quite strong. Alexander H. Everett, editor of *The North American Review,* may be taken as a typical example of some of the opposition to Transcendentalism. He traced its descent from idealism, which he called "an unsubstantiated dream" more suitable to the earlier stages of philosophy than to the present sophisticated age. Transcendentalism possessed the same ephemeral quality as the German idealism following Kant. This nebulous air was produced by an extremely vague, obscure vocabulary which few could understand.[36]

The Transcendentalists struck back at the Unitarians and started to develop their own brand of theology. They had become the new conservatives. Parker stated that the "liberal ministers," as he called the Unitarians, did not give enough credit to religious sentiment; their sermons related too often to outward things; their prayers were cold; and above all they were dismally lacking in piety.[37] A Calvinist might well have been satisfied with this criticism of Unitarianism.

The Transcendentalists did not find it difficult to criticize other groups, but they did find it difficult to make plans for cooperation among themselves. The first problem which faces any group just organizing is the definition of common ideals and goals. The problem was especially acute for the Transcendentalists since their language was so vague and their membership was comprised of so many independent thinkers.

---

[32] Perry Miller, *The Transcendentalists* (Cambridge: Harvard University, 1950), p. 46 (quoting Orestes Brownson's *The Convert*).

[33] Goddard, pp. 45-51.

[34] *Ibid.,* pp. 53-54.

[35] *Ibid.,* pp. 81-82.

[36] Miller, p. 32.

[37] Goddard, pp. 26-27.

George Ripley of Brook Farm fame set himself to define Transcendentalism. In a Boston sermon he characterized the Transcendentalists as a group of people who wished to reform the prevalent philosophy, who believed that truth could and did transcend the order of the external senses, whose main idea was that matter was inferior to mind, and who thought that the truthfulness of religion did not depend upon history or tradition but upon the verifying element within the soul.[38] Perhaps the essence of Ripley's definition was that the world was unified in God who was immanent in the world, and that each soul, since it contained the same elements, was one with the world soul.[39]

I have noted the Transcendentalist debt to idealism. But many elements of earlier thought can be recognized in the movement: the seventeenth-century religious faith based upon the awful mystery of God; the cult of reason of the eighteenth century which assumed nature to be entirely knowable; and the elevation of the sentiments in the nineteenth century due to romantic presuppositions.[40] All these ideas combined to form the four basic tenets of Transcendentalism. The first tenet was monism or the identity of the world and God; the second was the idea of microcosm or the incorporation in each entity of the laws and meanings of the entire universe; the third was the concept of macrocosm or the soul of man equalling the world soul; and the last was symbolism or spirit embodied and made visible in nature.[41]

Could people combine these tenets with traditional Christianity and remain within a Christian framework? The critical views coming from Transcendentalism might well strike at the very bases of orthodoxy. Many of the lesser known Transcendentalists were Unitarian ministers who tried to make an effective compromise between Unitarianism and Transcendentalism. These men assigned themselves the task of making religion philosophical and philosophy religious.[42]

Every group of thinkers that makes any serious attempt at consistency and continuity must operate with some assumption as to the nature of man upon which to posit institutional constructs. The Transcendentalists were no exception, although they were

---

[38] John Thomas Codman, *Brook Farm* (Boston: Arena, 1894), p. 4.

[39] Goddard, p. 4.

[40] Woodbridge Riley, *American Thought from Puritanism to Pragmatism and Beyond* (New York: Henry Holt, 1915), p. 140.

[41] *Ibid.*, pp. 142-43.

[42] Ronald V. Wells, *Three Christian Transcendentalists* (New York: Columbia University, 1943), pp. 2-3.

more interested in the religious consequences of human nature than in building an institutional framework. Assuming that man's nature was such that his sense of dependence upon God was innate, Theodore Parker eliminated the need for the authenticity of historic revelation.[43] In this definition man possessed all the necessary religious attributes without recourse to outside stimuli. One notes that the Calvinists had assumed human nature to be depraved and the Unitarians had asserted it to be essentially good, though still in need of outside help to secure religious truths. The Transcendentalists went a step further by asserting that man's nature almost partook of divinity.[44] Some confusion existed among Transcendentalists as to whether human nature was the possession of man collectively or individually. In general, they used the terms "man" and "the people" interchangeably when they spoke of the divine-human nature.[45]

Contemporary religious schools could be separated too by the attributes they assigned to man. What qualities did the Transcendentalists think man possessed? Emerson made a strong attempt to place man outside the conditioning factors of society, institutions, habits, ritual, custom, so as to find man's genius undetermined by any extraneous feature.[46] Having done this, Emerson found the prime factor in man's mind to be consciousness, an awareness of his own life, not careful, calculated thought swathed in layers of learning and socialization. Consciousness was guided, however, by certain other mental attributes of man, the major one being conscience.

Utilitarians, drawing on Lockean sensate psychology, had defined conscience as the body of rules that guided men toward happiness; but Transcendental thinkers rejected this view as inadequate. Conscience, they said, gave man an instant, intuitive knowledge of the motive for an act; it was the practical law of actions; and it was the correlative of God, a manifestation of God.[47] The nature of conscience was used by James Marsh, a leading Christian Transcendentalist, to define two other theological positions. Evangelical systems were based largely upon conscience, while pantheistic, natural ones were founded upon purely specula-

---

[43] Miller, p. 227.
[44] Goddard, p. 28.
[45] George Boaz, *Romanticism in America* (Baltimore: Johns Hopkins, 1940), p. 3.
[46] Lewis Mumford, *The Golden Age*, p. 96.
[47] Wells, pp. 42-43.

tive convictions.[48] Transcendentalism stood between these two extremes.

Another attribute which man possessed to aid his consciousness was reason. This faculty related intimately with conscience; but it was differentiated distinctly from understanding, as understanding merely drew conclusions from observed phenomena. By definition, understanding was a Lockean faculty that relied primarily on the senses, contrary to reason which was based upon intuition. Believing the mind had powers of its own, the New England thinkers discounted understanding and elevated reason. Theologically speaking, this was a reaction against all those who had denied the self-sufficiency of the human mind.[49] Elevating the faculty of reason also elevated the human mind. Reason, according to Marsh, was the basis for universal laws; it was "the integral spirit of a regenerated man, linking together sense, understanding, and imagination as three components"; and it was synonymous with being.[50]

One of the sources used by the Transcendentalists to support the power of reason was Swedenborg. Almost all of the Transcendentalists had been introduced to Swedenborgianism via a book written by Sampson Reed, a contemporary Swedenborgian. Concerned with the problem of knowledge, Reed entitled his book, *The Growth of the Mind*. His important contribution to Transcendentalism was his emphasis upon the fluidity of thought and his prediction that the next century would bring a great improvement in the science of mind.[51] Accepting this prediction as a challenge, the Transcendentalists strove to increase scientific knowledge about the mind.

In order to build a firm science of the mind, the Transcendentalists had to closely scrutinize prevailing assumptions. Lockean psychology and Scottish intuitionism were critically examined and found to be contributing to natural rather than spiritual religion. Both schools assumed that nature was necessitarian and the mind was passive, which meant that sense impressions were more important than reflection. The virtual enslavement of reason to sense was deemed extremely unfortunate by the Transcendentalists since they thought it handicapped faith.[52] The reconciliation of

---

[48] *Ibid.,* p. 163.
[49] Van Wyck Brooks, *The Flowering of New England,* p. 190.
[50] Wells, pp. 24-27.
[51] Kenneth Walter Cameron, *Emerson the Essayist,* Vol. II (Raleigh, North Carolina: Thistle Press, 1945), p. 13.
[52] Wells, pp. 22-23.

sense psychology with religious faith had been one of the more impressive intellectual feats of Calvinism but this compromise proved inadequate for the Transcendentalists.

Only a complete revolution would satisfy. Deductive reasoning was elevated over inductive reasoning. The Transcendentalists maintained that the laws of nature were found only by the process of introspection and not in the study of the external, material world. Material objects, therefore, lacked the reality of mind or soul.[53] Since the individual contained all the laws of the universe, it was easier to discover these laws through actions expressing the mind than by a detailed examination of the natural world. However much the Transcendentalists worshipped nature, they were not naturalists. Intuition and not sense impression unlocked the door to nature. Perhaps the most extreme expression of reliance upon reflection was a remark Bronson Alcott supposedly made: "O for the safe and natural way of intuition! I cannot grope like a mole in the gloomy passages of experience."[54] Since the external world was inferior to the internal one, the organs of sense collection were inferior to the workings of the mind. The organs of sense impression included memory, which was the produced effect of learning and was not to be confused with intuition.[55]

Intuition, reason, and conscience, which the Transcendentalists regarded as almost synonymous, furnished the reflective tools which indicated man's freedom. Since man alone possessed a self-determining will, he could become aware of himself and his goals. The power of free agency resulting from a self-determining will distinguished man from animal.[56] The faculty of reason gave man enormous power since the mind not only accounted for motives but also originated them. If man himself had never had power, he would not appreciate power in God, so man must have some power to be able to comprehend God. Furthermore, to deny man power would be to make God the only active agent and to destroy man's sense of responsibility.[57] The Transcendentalists believed man had the freedom and power to originate his own action and the force to carry it through, and that he was therefore responsible for this action.

Since responsibility for actions was a necessary corollary of

---

[53] Odell Shepard, *Pedlar's Progress* (Boston: Little, Brown, 1937), pp. 257-58.

[54] Goddard, p. 153.

[55] Cameron, p. 14.

[56] Wells, pp. 41-42.

[57] *Ibid.*, p. 154.

power to initiate these actions, moral choices were major concerns for the Transcendentalists, as they had been for the Unitarians and Calvinists. Perhaps their morality can be illustrated best by the lessons Alcott taught at his ill-fated Temple School. Although the Puritan ethic remained pervasive, there was none of the secularization of this ethic that had been present in Benjamin Franklin and Noah Webster.[58] Goodness was an end in itself, not to be striven for in the hope that tangible, material rewards might follow. Alcott equated the moral law with God, since both were discoverable by man's moral sense. This meant that the highest good and the most urgent duty of man was to use his freedom, power, and responsibility to obey the moral law written in his soul.

While introspection taught man more than any other technique did, sense experience was important too. The Transcendentalists believed that God was immanent in matter as well as in man.[59] Nature ran a close second to man in importance, for the virtue, beauty, truth, and goodness present in nature showed the individual the spirit of God who animates nature. Also, nature indicated to man by the mere fact of its existence that there was a creator who had made it.[60] Both man and nature reflected God.

Samuel Osgood, a Cincinnati Transcendentalist, expressed an opinion on nature which almost any Transcendentalist would accept. He observed the ideas about nature appearing in his society and found reason for optimism in those ideas. Before long, he thought, nature will be accorded a position commensurate with her worth, for more and more people are considering nature for her symbolic value in indicating God, His beauty, love, power, and wisdom, and not for her material worth.[61] Nature was assured a more permanent place in the value schemes of men, because nature, although regarded by many as ephemeral, was more real than other objects not containing the beauty and spirit of God. God and nature did not have reciprocal action, however, since the universe was produced by God and mirrored Him.[62]

A. Bronson Alcott held a view of nature common to most of the Transcendentalists: that the material world merely reflected the spiritual one, "that the outward world of time and space exists

---

[58] Shepard, p. 170.

[59] Miller, pp. 485-86 (quoting *Theodore Parker's Experience as a Minister*).

[60] Arthur M. Schlesinger, Jr., *Orestes A. Brownson: Pilgrim's Progress* (Boston: Little, Brown, 1939), pp. 231-32.

[61] Miller, p. 165.

[62] Wells, p. 29.

only as God's vast allegory, forever hinting at inward spiritual truth."[63] When nature was dissected by man's reason, its composition revealed two sections, the outward and the inward. The outer was substance and image, the inner was form and idea.[64] Only the inner gave shape and meaning, but the outer was important too, since it revealed the inner. Only through the medium of matter could sense impressions of spirit be made. Nature's physical state breaks the unity of God into a multiplicity of forms so that the mind, too feeble to grasp God's unity directly, can gain a hint of this unity by visualizing smaller bits of it in nature.[65]

The Transcendentalists had much to say about miracles. In the first place, they denied that miracles were necessary to substantiate the truth of Christianity; rather they held that only strong belief in Christianity supplied the faith necessary to accept miracles.[66] Remaining firmly within the main framework of Christian tradition, the Unitarians clashed directly with the Transcendentalists on this point. Miracles proved Christianity, said Andrews Norton, staunch Unitarian protagonist: Destroy miracles and you destroy Christianity.

Miracles occurred for the Unitarians in a mechanical universe in which natural laws operated and in which miracles could contradict these laws. The Transcendentalists denied the existence of such a mechanical world. Their view of the world made miracles, God's action, out of every natural event. An example of this view in practice was the Transcendental treatment of the miraculous events of Jesus' life. These events were accepted as probably true but as no more important than natural happenings.[67] The Transcendentalist world admitted, in fact, of no division into natural and supernatural.

A nature continually revealing God left, however, a small gap to be filled. This was done by institutions, which were designed to supplement nature by adjusting the less harmonious aspects of nature and man to each other. Harsh, unhospitable elements in both nature and man were smoothed over by institutions; these elements were the egotistical bias in man and the necessity of

---

[63] Shepard, p. 170 (quoting A. Bronson Alcott).

[64] Alcott's Diary, quoted in *Bronson Alcott's Fruitlands,* by Clara Endicott Sears (Boston: Houghton Mifflin, 1915), pp. 73-74.

[65] Odell Shepard, ed., *Journals of Bronson Alcott* (Boston: Little, Brown, 1938), p. 73.

[66] Wells, p. 210.

[67] *Ibid.,* p. 128.

physical existence in nature. Society curbed both of these aggressive forces.

The basic unit in society was the family, from which society proliferated into almost unbelievable complexity. The family symbolized creative power and spiritual generation and was the simple atom out of which the structure of society was built.[68] Since the family takes diverse elements and welds them together, it is a microcosm of society. It revealed too the manner in which society was formed. For like the family, society was comprised of individuals who assumed its bonds voluntarily.

Instead of being a mere collection of individuals and families, society was "an intimate union of individuals, voluntarily cooperating for the common good, actuated by social feelings, governed by social principles, and urged onward by social improvements."[69] Two elements were necessary for society, an aggregate of individuals and a common sense of cooperation. Both these elements had to be present before any group could be called a true society, but the individual was most important since his voluntary action held society together. If one followed this premise to its logical conclusion, an individual could destroy society by a withdrawal of his consent to cooperate.

Government, society, and the state were three different things, not to be confused. Government had no existence prior to its institution by society to do the bidding of society.[70] Since government was but a tool of society and since the best tool was the one which was flexible enough to conform to the needs of society, representative or democratic governments were the best. Presumably if government followed the laws of God or of the perfect society exactly, the kingdom of heaven would be set up on earth. The growth of increasingly representative institutions, reflecting the interests of mankind at large, was shown by history. History revealed too the supremacy of democratic institutions.

But a look at the contemporary scene revealed that the perfect society had not yet evolved; sin and error still existed in society as well as in the individual. Brownson, looking over contemporary society, concluded that slavery was an excellent example of institutionalized evil, since slavery was not produced by individuals then living but had been handed down through society.[71] Since

---

[68] Herbert Schneider, *A History of American Philosophy* (New York: Columbia University, 1946), p. 288.
[69] Miller, p. 73.
[70] *Ibid.*, pp. 440-41.
[71] Schlesinger, p. 79.

society needed redemption as badly as individuals did, Christianity, it was thought, ought to address itself to the task of saving society as well. If organized Christianity refused to accept this challenge, then perhaps it should be abandoned. George Ripley gave this as a reason for resigning the pastorate of a Unitarian group.[72]

The same force in man that worked for his salvation and made him join society also caused him to dabble in evil. Man's will might seek temporal gratifications in society instead of in goals dictated by universal law.[73] As an individual pursued increasingly selfish ends, he became more and more degraded. The societal result of this degradation was institutional evil, reflecting the evil of man. The institutional form of evil might last for some time after the individual evil which created it, but would inevitably die if individual evil died. Virtue might also become institutionalized and present a danger to man, for institutional virtue most often stressed the letter of the law to the detriment of the spirit. Society contributed little but evil to man.

The claims of society were relatively unimportant for the Transcendentalists. Even their famous venture at collectivism, Brook Farm, was atypical.[74] Reconciliation of individual elements with social processes remained secondary to the development of strong individualism. Perhaps the strongest attempt to find a meeting place for the individual and society was made by Bronson Alcott at his Temple School. There he emphasized that individual action involved social awareness. This was, no doubt, a concomitant of his belief that the moral life could be achieved by mutual effort.[75]

A more typical view of the interaction of the individual and society was presented in Transcendental aesthetics. Elizabeth Peabody, an associate of Alcott in his school, maintained that there were two steps to the achievement of true art. The first was the formation of a cultural base of common national and religious views, a characteristic romantic idea. Then, after a society possessed common ideals, the individual stepped in, cast off the bonds of society, and created superior, more refined, aesthetic concepts.[76] Although society was necessary, the individual was of primary importance. The Transcendentalists never doubted that society existed only for the benefit of the individual.

As I have indicated, the Transcendentalists believed that the

---

72 Miller, p. 256.
73 Wells, p. 47.
74 Goddard, pp. 7-8.
75 Odell Shepard, *Pedlar's Progress,* pp. 168-69.
76 Miller, p. 374.

rise of representative institutions exhibited progress in the world. This material progress, however, only symbolized internal, individual, moral progress. Since matter was the passive and spirit the impelling element in history, devotion to ideals of mind and spirit was devotion to the cause of progress and humanity.[77] As individuals improved themselves, so did they improve the world; such progress would result in the ultimate perfection of the human race. Hence moral progress was the significant progress.

It was the work of Christ, as interpreted in Christianity, that made progress possible. Saving men from the insufficiency of natural self-will, Christianity functioned to give men spiritual freedom. Christ's role was to give man "the spiritual necessities without which he can never achieve his true nature. Or, to put it another way, Christ fulfills the capacity in men for the reception of spiritual good."[78] The traditional notion of the atonement was changed by the Transcendentalists so that it connoted universal cleansing and purification. Atonement did not mean substitution for the punishment due a sinner nor would it lose its efficaciousness if no one accepted it.[79] The Transcendentalists defined salvation as the change from a natural to a spiritual nature, turning appetites and passions into good. In the end, then, the Transcendentalists turned to religion as the base upon which society and the individual rested; but this religion displayed peculiar qualities.

Theodore Parker classified religion into three subdivisions. The first was the natural or rationalistic view, holding that God created the world and then ceased to participate in it. He was not immanent in it, and man was able to know Him only by deducing Him from the sensations given off by the material world. This was obviously Deism. The second division included both Calvinism and Unitarianism. This was supernatural religion, characterized by some anti-rationalism and a belief in partial immanence: God revealed Himself in word and in miracles to certain men at certain places in the historic past. Finally, there existed the group in which Parker included himself, a group which tried to combine a firm reliance on reason with a belief in full immanence.[80]

All three of these religious schools existed in the world of Henry James, Sr. He could select elements of each.

---

[77] *Ibid.*, p. 427.
[78] *Ibid.*, p. 45.
[79] Wells, p. 47.
[80] Miller, pp. 316-321.

Two

Orthodox Swedenborgianism

Henry James's interest in Swedenborg was not unusual in his time. "Swedenborg was in the American and British air in the thirties and forties. Carlyle and Emerson and many others of a similar disposition read him and he was one of the many authors who contributed to the formation of the romantic mind."[1]

Emerson's statement that "the age is Swedenborg's" meant that the truth revealed by Swedenborg that the soul made its own environment, its own heaven and hell,[2] was particularly acceptable to Transcendentalists. For Emerson, the essence of Swedenborg's theology was the concept that man contained within himself a minute universe, revealed by his every idea and affection, and that, conversely, the universe, God, had the form of a great man.[3] Swedenborg maintained that God and man were quite similar in form and function, supporting Emerson's own impression of the divinity already inherent in man.

Also the elaboration by Swedenborg of the idea that the physical world mirrored the spiritual pleased Emerson.[4] Explaining as it did how the soul controls the body and spirit controls matter, the doctrine of correspondence was appreciated by the Transcendentalists, and Swedenborg gained credit for having had the prescience to have first discovered the idea. The Platonic element in Swedenborg appealed to the Transcendental idealistic bent.

---

[1] Clinton Hartley Grattan, *The Three Jameses* (London: Longmans, Green, 1932), p. 43.

[2] F. O. Matthiessen, *American Renaissance* (London: Oxford University, 1941), p. viii.

[3] Ralph Waldo Emerson, *Representative Men* (Boston: Houghton Mifflin, 1876), pp. 114-15.

[4] *Ibid.,* p. 117.

Emerson was not the only student of Swedenborg to openly express his admiration. Impressed with Swedenborg's comparison of the shape of the universe to that of a man, Alcott described the world as consisting of one vast spinal column.[5] While many of the other Transcendentalists incorporated much from Swedenborg's thought, few went so far as the Swedenborgians in adopting the minor tenets of Swedenborg. Margaret Fuller sensed the danger implicit in adulation and warned against it. She admitted the valuable insights of Swedenborg but deplored the exclusive reliance upon his words by his organized followers, for this, she said, led to bigotry.[6]

Even more certain in criticism was Emerson, who actually was quite impressed with Swedenborg. His criticism was typically Transcendental. First, Swedenborg had erred in assuming one material symbol for each spiritual truth when he should have been occupying his time with the discovery of universal symbols. This was, however, a common fault among men of genius, especially those who created original systems of thought.[7] Secondly, Swedenborg demonstrated by his refusal to admit the possibility of conversion for evil spirits that he retained remnants of Gothic theology.[8]

These exceptions were minor, however, when compared to the major criticism of Swedenborg. Given the common assumptions of Emerson and the Transcendentalists, a large deficiency in Swedenborg's thought could be pointed out, a deficiency common to eighteenth-century thinkers. The world system of Swedenborg was not a spontaneous, living organism; the universe was described as a crystal with all components in their static, ordered places. Any element of life which might have been injected into this universe by man was lacking, for Swedenborg had discounted the power of will as man's motivating force.[9] Emerson, in common with the other Transcendentalists, assumed that the world was given life by the presence of man and that without this presence the world would lose its meaning. The value of the individual in Transcendental mind is nowhere more emphatically stated than in Emerson's criticism of Swedenborg.

The basic underevaluation of man's part in the world scheme

---

[5] Goddard, *Studies in New England Transcendentalism,* p. 130.

[6] Margaret Fuller Ossoli, *Works of Margaret Fuller* (Boston: Roberts Brothers, 1875), p. 338.

[7] Matthiessen, *American Renaissance,* pp. 42-43.

[8] *Ibid.,* p. 138.

[9] Emerson, *Representative Men,* p. 133.

contributed to other mistakes. One was that the symbol for the expression of Swedenborg's thought was not the widest which he could have chosen. He attached his thought to the Christian symbol, a necessarily restrictive one, when he should have used the moral sentiment, a symbol large enough to contain many theological systems. Man and his moral freedom were more important than any system, so the freedom of man was the vital element to be stressed.[10]

One final example of the contrast of ideas between the sage of the eighteenth and the sage of the nineteenth centuries was that of Swedenborg's concept of marriages in heaven. Emerson was, of course, opposed to the idea. This opposition was not startling in itself, since many critics of Swedenborg had attacked the institution of celestial wedlock. The interesting feature of Emerson's rejection, however, was the fundamental postulate upon which it was based. Starting with a definition of celestial love as a similar perception of truths, Emerson denied the possibility of ever achieving a true celestial marriage. If marriage were to exist eternally, heaven must be assumed to be static. This, Emerson stated, was impossible. Since one of the attributes of man was his continual discovery of new truths, a celestial marriage would dissolve when a new truth was discovered by one partner in heaven. Even in heaven every individual was essentially alone as "all loves and friendships are momentary."[11] Even the comfort of heavenly marriage was denied by Emerson in the interest of the continually growing individual.

The influence of Swedenborg went beyond the Transcendentalists to those who determined to follow the lead of Swedenborg in religious affairs to the exclusion of all others. The Swedenborgian influence had come to America late in the eighteenth century, only a short time after the death of Swedenborg. Originally, no separate Swedenborgian church existed since most of Swedenborg's followers clung to the hope of converting the entire Christian world. Since the converts believed, as did Swedenborg, that the last judgment had already taken place, the influx of heavenly light and warmth must be flowing into all hearts and minds and not into exclusively Swedenborgian ones.[12] The Swedenborgians were, like almost all new religious movements, more inclusive than exclusive, hoping in a completely new world.

---

[10] *Ibid.*, p. 135.

[11] *Ibid.*, p. 128.

[12] Benjamin F. Barrett, *The Golden Reed* (New York: D. Appleton, 1855), p. 306.

As time went on, however, the Swedenborgians proceeded to become an organized sect. This was shown best by the increase in size of the New Church. In 1820 there were, according to the available statistics, twelve societies, eight ordained ministers, and two hundred thirty members.[13] The Census of 1830 in America showed twenty-eight societies, sixteen ministers, five hundred members, and seven temples, as their church buildings were called.[14] In ten years the size of the sect had almost doubled. By 1840 the number of members had increased to eight hundred fifty, while the number of ministers had increased to twenty and the number of societies had decreased to twenty.[15] Lay leadership in the New Church was passing into the hands of professional ministers. In 1850 the United States Census indicated that the New Church had fourteen hundred fifty members, thirty-two ministers, and fifty-four societies.[16] The membership had approximately doubled every ten years over a thirty-year span.

The works of Swedenborg had come to America and were read. Occasionally ministers and members of other denominations would obtain these books, read them, and become convinced of their truth. As is the case with the reception of new ideas, an attempt was made at first to fit these new concepts into old frameworks. This was not always possible, so the New Church gained when other denominations refused to allow Swedenborgian ideas to infiltrate. Several examples can be given. Reverend William Bird of Boston, a Baptist minister, suffered excommunication by the Baptists, whereupon he became a Swedenborgian.[17] In 1822 Reverend Manning B. Roche, an Episcopal minister who openly avowed Swedenborgian ideas, was attacked by another Episcopal minister and was forced to resign. He promptly became a Swedenborgian minister.[18] In Abington, Massachusetts, Reverend Holland Weeks, a Presbyterian minister, began to preach Swedenborgian doctrine and was, as a result, regularly tried for heresy and forced out of the church.[19] Sometimes a minister succeeded in preaching Swedenborgianism without ever changing denominational titles; some, like Reverend Boyle of the Free-Will Baptists,

---

[13] Carl Theophilis Odhner, *Annals of the New Church, 1688-1850*, I (Bryn Athyn, Pa.: Academy of the New Church, 1904), pp. 277-78.

[14] *Ibid.*, p. 364.

[15] *Ibid.*, p. 449.

[16] *Ibid.*, p. 566.

[17] *Ibid.*, p. 365.

[18] *Ibid.*, p. 296.

[19] *Ibid.*, pp. 278-79.

persuaded a portion of their parish members to become Sweden-borgians with them.[20] No more lucid illustration is needed than that the formation of a sect was in progress. Original ideas appear which first seem to be assimilated into the hierarchical structures, but after a short time the holders of these ideas are forced out of these old structures into new ones which institutionalize those ideas. Since it was becoming increasingly difficult to remain within traditional denominations and sects, voluntary dissociation from these institutions occurred and association with new, sympathetic ones followed. Ecclesiastical histories abound in such cases.

What ideas had such strong appeal for proselytes? One of them was the New Church emphasis upon the power of man and de-emphasis upon the arbitrary ordinances of God. From the formation of the first society in Baltimore in 1792 the revolt against certain elements of Calvinism appeared. Thus, Christian Kramer, one of the original members in the United States, came to Swedenborgianism via a revolt against the doctrine of predestination.[21] The more positive ideas of Swedenborg also attracted John Perry, a Congregational minister, who became convinced, after studying the Bible, that God was unitary and that man was early resurrected from the body.[22] The problem of life after death concerned Francis Phelps, another converted member. After reading Sampson Reed's *Concerning Marriages in Heaven,* he decided that Swedenborg's ideas could best inform him of what happened after death, since other Christian groups denied that anything specific could be known about the life hereafter.[23] The concern of many people with the next life seemed to have been common in the first half of the eighteenth century and was responsible for bringing members into the New Church. One such new member was enrolled after "he commented on a lately deceased friend, expressed interest in his present condition, and wondered what he was doing in the other world."[24] Showing the most concern about life after death, the parents of two recently deceased children came to the New Church after having had the misfortune to hear their own Calvinist minister state his considered opinion that the streets of hell were paved with the bones

[20] *Ibid.,* p. 279.
[21] Ednah C. Silver, *Sketches of the New Church* (Boston: The Massachusetts New Church Union, 1920), p. 39.
[22] *Ibid.,* pp. 90-91.
[23] *Ibid.,* pp. 86-87.
[24] *Ibid.*

of unredeemed infants.[25] It is hardly surprising to note that these two became Swedenborgians.

These few examples were designed to show the impulses that drew new members into the Swedenborgian fold. These reasons were quite similar to the ones other people used to justify their desertion of old churches and entrance into new ones. Two of the excuses given were a disgust with the seemingly irrational elements of the Christian faith as held by the Calvinists — infant damnation, original sin, and predestination — and also a concern with an elaboration of the future life and of the possibility of attaining it. The converts to the New Church became members for the same reasons that others were becoming Unitarians and Campbellites.

One of the most important steps in the founding of a new sect is to indicate that the founder had divine inspiration. From the original position that this particular individual had extremely incisive insights the idea gradually evolves that everything that he said and did was a product of direct inspiration from God. One of the later American Swedenborgians wrote coldly of Mrs. Eddy and her spiritual interpretation of the world, one similar in many ways to Swedenborg's, claiming that Swedenborg retained the traditional Christian duality between the worlds of spirit and matter and indicating that "her [Mrs. Eddy] claims to divine inspiration are naturally repellent to a church which has its *own* divinely inspired founder."[26] When the founder of a sect has become a saint, the institution has arrived.

The doctrines of the New Church as they evolved in America bore striking resemblances to those of the rational religions of the time. It was no accident that many former Unitarians could be found in Swedenborgian ranks. Assuming that men were free and rational, the church remained flexible enough to adapt its teaching to these attributes.[27] The church did not substitute faith for understanding, since the church frowned upon the acceptance of any idea that could not be rationally understood.[28] For the Swedenborgians all truth represented some law, natural or spiritual, which had to be understood to be obeyed. The mysterious Christian doctrines seemed to be eliminated.

But religion was in itself higher than reason. Intellectual agree-

[25] *Ibid.,* pp. 275-76.
[26] Marguerite B. Block, *The New Church in the New World* (New York: Henry Holt, 1932), p. 169.
[27] Barrett, p. 14.
[28] *Ibid.,* p. 16.

ment among men might have been a satisfactory basis for natural religion, but it was inadequate for the Swedenborgians. Union with God was less dependent upon reason than upon the possession of the right kind of emotions, as the things man loved were more important than the thoughts he had, willing and acting were superior to thinking.[29] In a certain limited sense, this was similar to Transcendental ideas, although the Transcendentalists phrased and defined their ideas more sharply.

The most important knowledge to be possessed about a man or a church was, therefore, not what either of them accomplished but the end each had in mind. Since the goal revealed the true dimensions of an individual or institution, the end determined the worth of each of these.[30] From this followed the assumption that false doctrine did not damn a person, providing, of course, that this person had the elements of divine love operating within him.[31] A true church would not demand unanimity of doctrine; wide diversity of opinion would be tolerated since truth's natural form varied. An individual would qualify as a member even if he had false ideas, as long as he possessed the spirit of charity.[32] All of the toleration shown reflected the belief that Christianity was not a creed but rather a formula for life itself. While the church held that error was no grounds for guilt or expulsion from the church, it also made it clear that error was not to be continued,[33] especially if this error came from evil living, ignorance, or false teachings.

While this liberal formulation seemed to be the opposite of sectarian narrowness, certain movements within Swedenborgianism belied this. One good example was the growing practice of requiring ordination of ministers. Any Protestant group has a difficult enough time in determining the leaders and teachers to unify the group, holding, as most of them do, that man is himself both priest and king and rejecting almost all authority save that of conscience. On the other hand, some organized leadership was necessary in order to aid the promulgation of true doctrine.

The first ordination among American Swedenborgians occurred in 1798 when two men were initiated into the priesthood by the two elders of the New Church in Baltimore.[34] This did not, how-

29 *Ibid.*
30 *Ibid.*, p. 270.
31 *Ibid.*, p. 102.
32 *Ibid.*, pp. 79-80.
33 *Ibid.*, p. 175.
34 Odhner, pp. 189-190.

ever, end the practice of extemporaneous preaching and administration of sacraments by lay leaders. The first step toward the regulation of the ministry was taken in the Second General Conference, when it was decided that neither the church in Philadelphia nor the one in Baltimore would ordain new ministers without the unanimous consent of the ministers of both.[35] The distinction of pastor from laity was still not complete, however. By 1821 the assumption persisted, as confirmed by committee findings, that ministers could possess secular occupations as well as their pastoral duties and that each society could draw up its own rules regulating ministerial selection and confirmation.[36]

There was considerable resistance to even a slight bent toward professional clergy. In 1824 the Cincinnati Society produced a letter written by one Daniel Roe "denying *in toto* the use of ordination or of any distinctive priesthood, and requesting the Convention to express itself upon the subject. . . ."[37] The furor this letter provoked began a controversy over the existence, nature, and duties of an organized pastoral caste, one which lasted almost a quarter of century. Opposition to a professional class of ministers was not inconsiderable all during the dispute.

The convention, as the highest official organ of the church, did not cease its attempts to acquire more power. From 1826 onward the ordaining power lay in the convention's hand from which it was channeled to local churches throughout the area, utilizing local ministers only as instruments.[38] This power was more legal than actual, however, as was illustrated in the 1830's by the difficulties with the so-called "conjugal-heresy" or "Boston principle." Originating in Boston in the agile mind of a student at Harvard Divinity School, the "Boston principle" stated that the relationship between a pastor and his congregation partook of the marriage relationship even to the point of being indissoluble except by death. For all practical purposes a pastor and his church were married, so that neither, as long as the other existed, could select another partner without being guilty of spiritual adultery.[39] If this movement were to be successful, effective central control by the convention would be stymied. Even though the movement failed, it blocked the consolidating tendencies for a considerable length of time.

---

[35] *Ibid.,* p. 264.
[36] *Ibid.,* p. 287.
[37] *Ibid.,* p. 312.
[38] *Ibid.,* p. 327.
[39] Block, p. 190.

By 1830 three distinct degrees of ministry had been created; these were ministers, pastors, and ordinary ministers.[40] The first order baptized new members into the church. Men in the second preached sermons, served as missionaries, and performed marriage ceremonies. The last group served primarily as ordainers of the first two orders. The lowest grade, ministers, tended to be the least professional while the other two grades were more often composed of career men. So it was indicative of the increasing conservatism of the Swedenborgians when, in 1848, they abolished the degree of minister.[41] The trend to a professional class had not been reversed and the New Church was becoming more rigid in its requirements.

Another problem confronting the New Church was the one of membership. What was to be the determinant of membership? Swedenborgians held, doctrinally speaking, that two sacraments, baptism and Holy Supper, were of significance. Both of these sacraments were symbolic,[42] a view shared by most Protestant sects. However, the sacraments were the divinely ordained means for gaining salvation, even though they could be administered by members of the laity. Therefore, their validity did not depend upon the faith or the reputation of the administration.[43] Given the conflicting views of the importance of the sacraments, would it be necessary to be baptized for admission into the fellowship of the New Church?

From the very beginning this was a knotty question, as many convinced Swedenborgians had come from other faiths in which they had been baptized. Was rebaptism necessary? In 1816 the practice of rebaptism was obligatory in the Baltimore Society, was optional in Philadelphia, and was rejected in New England and New York.[44] The convention had originally taken the position that anyone who signed the articles of faith was entitled to membership within the church without rebaptism. The history of the practice was contradictory for the next several years. By 1838 rebaptism was made obligatory, but ten years later the control was relaxed so that individual ministers and societies could do as they pleased. However, in another ten years the rule was obligatory again, making membership dependent upon re-

---

40 Odhner, pp. 428-29.
41 *Ibid.*, p. 558.
42 Barrett, p. 237.
43 *Ibid.*, p. 239.
44 Odhner, p. 249.

baptism.[45] The consolidation into a more restrictive society was not to be denied.

Besides the institutional tendencies shown by professional ordained ministers and the tightening membership qualifications, competing movements forced the Swedenborgians into a closer, more homogenous group. An example of the possibility of conflicting loyalties was given by a Swedenborgian society near Canton, Ohio, which became imbued with the principles of Fourierism and set up a communistic "phalanx."[46] This community eventually dissolved but not without causing much consternation. Since several of Fourier's ideas paralleled those of Swedenborg, these collectivistic ideas were especially attractive. Fourier emphasized a moral code and brotherhood, both good Christian virtues, so the fascination of Fourier was not difficult to understand. In order to minimize the danger of being absorbed into Fourierism New Church members received warnings against too close cooperation with Fourierism.

Two other movements attracted Swedenborgian attention. Both these movements were connected with the medicine of the time, one with a physical and the other with a mental orientation. Phrenology claimed a large amount of support in the early and mid-nineteenth century. The so-called science of determining man's mental and spiritual capacity by a study of the conformation of the head implied an all-embracing, mechanistic world view which ought to be guarded against. Homeopathy, the curing of disease by specific remedies, might also partake of the nature of a pseudoreligion. Many Swedenborgians were prominent in both movements, so the dangers of becoming too close were quite real. These movements, however, did not gain enough strength to take precedence over the more important doctrines of the church.

The attractions of outside, similar movements were not the only perils. The seeds of inner schism might always be present, as shown by the outbreak of seemingly heretical ideas in the fifties. This outbreak was known as the Academy Movement, one which finally succeeded in splitting the church some forty years later. In a sense, the movement was merely a logical culmination of the progress toward sectarian exclusiveness. The academy group had several tenets: the infallibility of Swedenborg, the literal truth of every divinely inspired word, an exclusive church, social life, priesthood, and education.[47] Quoting Sweden-

---

[45] Block, pp. 186-89.
[46] Odhner, p. 509.
[47] Block, p. 205.

borg to the effect that man might be allowed concubines before he found his true spiritual mate, the Academy Movement maintained that the possession of a concubine was not cause for dismissal from the church, even for a minister.[48] While the Academy never captured the church, it was powerful enough to exert considerable influence.

The sectarian impulse of the Swedenborgians was rejected by two groups of liberal Swedenborgians, one of these groups being composed primarily of Henry James, Sr., and a few devoted disciples, who spoke for a renewed, universal, humanitarian religion, and the other a group composed of those who emphasized the more esoteric spiritual science.[49] Both liberal elements of Swedenborgians wished to reverse the sectarian trend and to establish a more universal organization.

Henry James, Sr., took the middle way between those who thought Swedenborg's writings should be manifest in the narrow, institutional, sectarian form and those Transcendentalists who criticized Swedenborg for his de-emphasis of human will. Between these two formulations and with the tradition of Calvinist, Unitarian, and Transcendental Christianity behind and around him, James hammered out his own peculiar interpretation of Swedenborg and applied this interpretation to a criticism and evaluation of contemporary society.

---

[48] *Ibid.*, p. 222.

[49] Herbert W. Schneider and George Lawton, *A Prophet and a Pilgrim* (New York: Columbia University, 1942), pp. 21-22.

Three

Basic Religious Premises

Henry James was raised in the bosom of orthodoxy, his family observing the letter of Puritan morality. This upbringing may partially explain James's later revulsion against those pious Sabbatarians who made every Sunday such a dull, lifeless affair for a young boy. He wanted a living faith and was given a dying one. However, from the very beginning of his life until the end of it, James surrounded himself with religious ideas. Religion was his life. His social and political philosophies were secondary to his religious views and were, most frequently, products of those views. The assumptions that are the keystone to his whole system, if his body of thought can be said to have enough unity to constitute a system, are religious.

James came from a family that had Presbyterian convictions. So when he expressed the desire to enter the ministry, he was sent to the seminary at Princeton in 1835. Two and a half years later he left, saying that the atmosphere was becoming too stultifying and that being separated from the world and splitting theological hairs was emotionally inadequate. Princeton, it must be remembered, was the stronghold of religious conservatism at this time. Most of the Calvinist legacy of the seventeenth and eighteenth centuries was inherited by orthodox Presbyterianism, especially since Unitarianism and Arminianism infected New England Congregationalism. James's educational heritage was, therefore, the strict Calvinism of an orthodox Presbyterian, with its emphasis upon original sin and a just, omnipotent God.

Shortly after leaving the seminary at Princeton, James encountered a group following the teachings of a certain Robert Sandeman. Radically different from the Presbyterians at Princeton, the Sandemanians preached a return to a church fellowship like that of the early Christians. This involved the practice of a rather close fellowship combined with an active lay participation in the organization and activities of the church. The members served voluntarily, without pay, and dispensed with professional clergy. More important, the Sandemanians held as a corollary to their belief that salvation came only through grace and not through any attempts at moral behavior, a form of antinomianism which contradicted almost all of the traditional notions of divine election.[1] In common with Calvinism it emphasized the powerful nature of God in contrast to the weakness of man. The Sandemanians displayed all of the exclusiveness characteristic of sects, so James never became active in this group even though he was deeply impressed by it.

The most powerful influence on James's thought was, however, Swedenborgianism. In many ways James merely reshifted and reevaluated Swedenborg to produce a similar system.

Emmanuel Swedenborg was a Swedish theologian and scientist born in 1688, son of a prominent Lutheran minister who was royal chaplain to Charles X and was ennobled by Queen Ulrica Eleanora. Swedenborg studied at Upsala University, concentrating upon the natural sciences, which he pursued further at London, Leyden, and Paris. Upon returning to Sweden, he became Extraordinary Assessor of the Councils of Mines. He performed quite capably as an engineer and mining expert, writing several volumes on these subjects, the ones on metallurgy gaining him scientific recognition. He next turned to his first love, the biological sciences, investigating and studying anatomy, physiology, and psychology. But in 1744 he came into contact with a group of Moravians and experienced a deep conviction of sin. His interest in biology was replaced by a religious concern. The result was a series of religious books, starting with the publication of the first volume of *Arcana Caelestia* in 1749. Until his death in 1771, Swedenborg remained as engrossed in religious affairs as he had previously been in scientific ones.

Swedenborg tried to apply to religion those methods that had proved so successful for him in the scientific field. His goal was nothing less than to make out of the facts of life, as explained by reason, a science of theology that was capable of satisfying the needs of life.[2] This theology revealed platonic and neo-pla-

---

[1] Austin Warren, *The Elder Henry James* (New York: Macmillan, 1934), pp. 32-37.

[2] George Trowbridge, *Swedenborg* (New York: The Swedenborg Foundation, Incorporated, 1920), p. 120.

tonic influences, for Swedenborg had strongly idealistic tendencies. He believed that there was but one substance, God, which permeated the world, including men and angels,[3] giving form and direction to the entire universe. Since Swedenborg thought that the world could best be understood in terms of the substance that gave it being, he might justly be called a spiritual monist. Again the emphasis upon the power of God can be noted in Swedenborg's thought, as in the other religious thought that impressed James. Swedenborg also attempted to enlist science to support religion, an idea James found very attractive.

It is a matter of conjecture exactly how much James owed to Swedenborg. William Dean Howells was of the opinion that James was a thoroughgoing Swedenborgian.

> But Henry James was incommensurably more Swedenborgian than either of us [Howells and Boyesen, a Norwegian Swedenborgian]: he lived and thought and felt Swedenborg with an entirety and intensity far beyond the mere assent of other men.[4]

We also have the witness of Henry James, Jr. In his *Notes of a Son and Brother,* he mentions that his father would often indicate his ideas simply by saying that he was a follower of Swedenborg. He remembered his father's defending Swedenborg rather vigorously, once attacking someone who maintained that Swedenborg was hardly credible with the flat statement that Swedenborg was "insipid with veracity."[5]

Yet James was never formally a member of the New Church in America; in fact, he attacked both the church and its erstwhile members quite violently. J. J. Garth Wilkinson, one of the more acute English Swedenborgians, insisted that James should forbear from calling himself a Swedenborgian because of the fundamental incompatibility of his ideas with those of Swedenborg.[6] In particular, Wilkinson thought James's concept of the Divine-Natural-Humanity, the central theme of his work, a gross perversion of Swedenborg. Swedenborg, he maintained, had used this idea to signify God's triumph in Christ, while James believed that God

---

[3] Emmanuel Swedenborg, *True Christian Religion* (New York: American Swedenborg Printing and Publishing Society, 1898), p. 26.

[4] William Dean Howells, *Literary Friends and Acquaintances* (New York: Harper and Brothers, 1900), p. 266.

[5] Henry James, Jr., *Notes of a Son and Brother* (New York: Charles Scribner's Sons, 1914), pp. 157-58.

[6] Ralph Barton Perry, *The Thought and Character of William James,* I (Boston: Little, Brown, 1935), pp. 26-27.

merged with humanity through Christ.[7] Wilkinson's view is, I think, not without justice.

Frederick Young, the most recent critic of the elder James, holds that James differed from Swedenborg in two significant ways, both of which were a product of James's encounter with Sandeman-ianism. Young traces the antinomianism and anti-ecclesiasticism in James to Sandeman, who valued the Gospel over the moral law and the church. These views, Young asserts, are not to be found in Swedenborg; instead Swedenborg took pains to attack such doctrines.[8]

Young's analysis, however, hardly seems defensible. First, what antinomian tendencies James had were certainly shared by Swe-denborg. James never advocated anything but genuinely moral behavior; what he did object to was moral behavior generated by pride. Swedenborg too objected to morality for the sake of reputation and believed that men who were moral but lacked faith were lost.[9] Furthermore, Swedenborg pictured the church in a typically mystical fashion when he said it was composed of the persons in whom Christ dwelled.[10] The conception of the church as the body of all believers could have led Swedenborg to anti-ecclesiastical tendencies, as it had other Christian mystics. The point here is not that Swedenborg and James held the same theological position, but that there was nothing in James that could not have been developed from Swedenborg.

James never took Swedenborg on faith alone; he was too chary of dogmatics to do that. Swedenborg, to be sure, did not require this, for he was so loath to be demanding that he made no attempt to convince anyone of the truth of his ideas or visions. No one seeking an infallible guide would be attracted to Swedenborg.[11] Expressing the view that Swedenborg might have done well to explain and interpret his ideas rather than to present so much unprocessed raw material, James assumed the role of interpreter in lieu of Swedenborg's own interpretation.

James tried to define his debt to Swedenborg as clearly as possible. He agreed that Swedenborg's attempt to formulate a theological science was worthwhile, although he did find the name somewhat unsuitable. He also agreed with Swedenborg's method

---

[7] *Ibid.*

[8] Frederick Harold Young, *The Philosophy of Henry James, Sr.* (New York: Bookman Associates, 1951), p. 61.

[9] Swedenborg, *True Christian Religion*, p. 409.

[10] *Ibid.*, p. 394.

[11] James, as quoted in Warren, *The Elder Henry James*, p. 61.

in setting up an all-embracing cosmology. The method did not involve a denial of sense impressions, but relegated these impressions to a secondary position, placing the rational factor which organized sense impressions first.[12] This rational element was what had commended Swedenborg to James and was the bond that tied them together. As long as James knew Swedenborg was using this method, he viewed his findings with sympathy, even when he could not agree with his conclusions.[13]

James's definition of religion was not a commonly held one. Religion was not for him a system to be explained and elaborated; it was an attitude, almost an instinct. It was a feeling, engendered by conscience, of abject unworthiness, of separation from God because of sinfulness. This sense was so powerful that any sacrifice, even life itself, might be tolerated in order to return to divine favor.[14] All the myths and constructions of institutional religion had arisen from a need to placate this religious feeling. These had been attacked by science, and science had won out, for it was a product of man's rational mind. But by *his* definition of religion James could maintain that science and religion were not antagonistic, since science had only smashed the product of religion and not religion itself. The destruction of religious institutions had been almost completed by his day, James maintained, and the task to which he addressed himself was the satisfaction of the religious impulse without the institutional background. This was to be accomplished by philosophy, the positive counterpart of the negative function of science, that is, a creative, rational approach to the world and God.[15]

James was trying no less than the fusion of religious sentiment with science, which had destroyed the superficial, unnecessary manifestations of religion to form a new philosophy. The peculiar combination of religion and philosophy which James advocated was most sharply delineated by his son, Henry James, Jr., who described his religion as philosophy containing all the elements necessary for an explanation of the world and the forces, personal and impersonal, operating within that world. All this

[12] Henry James, "Swedenborg as a Theologian," *Massachusetts Quarterly Review* (1848), p. 293.

[13] Henry James, *The Secret of Swedenborg* (Boston: Fields, Osgood, 1869), p. 214.

[14] William James, ed., *The Literary Remains of Henry James* (Cambridge: University Press, 1884), p. 47.

[15] Henry James, *Substance and Shadow* (Boston: Tichnor and Fields, 1863), p. 454.

was done in a very personal, original, and complex manner.[16] James's combination of religion with science to create philosophy seems reminiscent of Comte's three stages of knowledge, which, however, ended in sociology instead of philosophy. This is not surprising since James had read Comte, although he was not impressed by him.

The religious sense of sinfulness described by James was experienced in his youth and became an impelling factor in his later religious development. He revealed a tender conscience at an early age. When he was still quite young, he had thrown snowballs at a younger brother to prevent the boy from following him to play. This trivial incident had, James said, the power "to keep me awake all night, bedewing my pillow with tears, and beseeching God to grant me forgiveness."[17] This same sense of sin remained with James throughout his life, growing no less vivid but becoming more sophisticated and socialized. When James considered his existence, he felt damned, for his life seemed a perversion of divine justice. Although he had all the advantages of inherited wealth, he was not one whit better mentally or spiritually than those less fortunate members of society who had to struggle for the bare necessities of life.[18]

Many men in the history of religion shared a conviction of deep, abiding sin and guilt. The reaction that this guilty feeling most often produced, however, was a search that ended in a feeling of election, of salvation in God's grace. James reacted differently, as he analyzed the consciousness of sin and reduced it to terms with which he could more readily cope.

The traditional Christian definition of sin, especially as selected and emphasized by Calvinist thought, divided sin into two categories, personal sin that man does and universal sin in which man shares. The latter was called original sin, coming from Adam and remaining as a burden on the rest of humanity. The idea of original sin was disturbing to James; it seemed to him to cut man off from all knowledge and hope of God. That God hated personal sin was understandable, but that God hated all men or human nature would make God a malignant creator.[19]

Rebelling against the hopelessness that a conception of original

---

16 Henry James, Jr., *Notes of a Son and Brother*, p. 164.

17 Henry James, *Lectures and Miscellanies* (New York: J. S. Redfield, 1852), p. 411.

18 Henry James, *The Secret of Swedenborg*, p. 173.

19 Henry James, *Society the Redeemed Form of Man* (Boston: Houghton, Osgood, 1879), p. 317.

sin initiated, James reexamined the relationship between God and man. He believed that evil was bad; and yet, to recognize oneself a sinner, to have the sense of having done wrong, was, he thought, the "height of man's spiritual achievement, for this world at all event."[20] How could he reconcile the fact that doing evil was bad with the fact that feeling guilty was the instrument for spiritual growth? James tended to relieve man of responsibility for sin, while insisting that the idea of being a sinner was primary for any kind of spiritual life. Again, this was not a new concept in Christian thought, having been present even among the early apostles.

As a sinner convicted by himself, James returned to a consideration of God to find the reason for the disparity between man and God. James never doubted the existence of God, for the presence of man proved to him the presence of God. God was the object of which man was the subject. But God must be defined to be understood. James quarreled with orthodox theology on the doctrine of inherent evil in man. If God and man were composed of two different substances, one good and the other evil, the two would never be reconciled. For as long as God was outside of man with differing interests from man and demanding absolute obedience from him in order to flatter Himself, man must hate God as God must hate man.[21]

James started with the assumption that the orthodox dichotomy between God and man was wrong, that there was no quarrel between them. Since James's fundamental axiom was the existence of God who was the sole possessor of being or life, man can only be the image of life or being.[22] With this idea James reveals a rather advanced spiritual monism, quite similar to that of Swedenborg. It followed then that God and man were fundamentally allied, that man, by his acts, could not offend God or be separated from Him.[23] The idea that God had any personal quarrel with men or would be concerned with moral conduct was preposterous.[24] This meant that man need no longer fear separation from God by some quality in his nature, tangible or intangible, that repelled God. One cannot hate one's own nature, and so God could not hate man, since man partook of God's own nature.

---

[20] Henry James, *Substance and Shadow,* pp. 180-81.
[21] Henry James, *Lectures and Miscellanies,* p. 240.
[22] Henry James, *Moralism and Christianity* (New York: J. S. Redfield, 1850), p. 5.
[23] Henry James, *Lectures and Miscellanies,* pp. 416-17.
[24] William James, p. 222.

Furthermore, God could be understood best in terms of human personality. When man conceives of God, said James, he thinks of an ideal man, of human qualities refined to perfection:[25]

> His being or perfection is not physical, but spiritual or human. He is not a fact, but the truth of all facts. He is not a thing, but the life of all things. His power consequently is not physical or muscular, since this is a power strictly finite, being measured by obstacles, but spiritual, or the power of Goodness and Truth. It does not descend to compete with human sinews, nor does it envy the tiger his victorious spring. It is not exerted mechanically or as an outward force — in which case of course it would immediately disqualify all the forces of nature, and swallow them up — but dynamically, as the force of an inward or spiritual life.[26]

God contained many features attractive to James, not for what He was but for what was implicit in Him. James was always quick to assert the spiritual nature of God and to de-emphasize His material force. Implying perfection, God's spiritual nature was indispensable in James's religious system, for this perfection allowed certain other worthwhile qualities, which James considered necessary, to come into existence.

James, as I have stated before, was concerned with his feeling of inadequacy, his sense of sin and guilt. Therefore, it was imperative for him to assume that God's perfection involved certain responsibilities toward man. God was under obligation to man, for He had allowed His creature some claims upon Him. This obligation was to allow man to share His attributes, especially the most important of them, His perfection.[27]

God's perfection was not absolute, however. James indicated that he took it to be relative, which meant that it was an active rather than a passive virtue. God had to be creative in order to mirror His own perfection, since His perfection was "entirely inseparable save in thought from the work of his hands."[28] God existed insofar as He was always active, always striving to create. The upshot of the necessary activity on the part of God was the continuous act of creation. Another corollary was that a creature, man, was necessary to make God's creativity possible. Man was as essential to God as God was to man.

---

[25] Henry James, *Lectures and Miscellanies,* p. 59.

[26] Henry James, *The Nature of Evil* (New York: D. Appleton, 1855), pp. 292-93.

[27] *Ibid.,* p. 46.

[28] Henry James, *The Secret of Swedenborg,* p. 179.

If the attributes of God seem familiar, it is not difficult to discover why. God contained all the virtues of a perfect man; God was the great man. This was not to be construed in the anthropomorphic sense that God was actually a material person to be worshipped; rather God possessed only spiritual virtues. The material side of God was present in man, since man gave form to spiritual virtues. Therefore man must strive to return his material form to a state equal to God, active, virtuous, and perfect. Swedenborg had maintained that the Last Judgment had already taken place, having occurred in 1756. The judgment was spiritual and marked, as he said, "the consummation of the age."[29] From that time onward larger numbers of people have been turning directly to God and entering into either heaven or hell. James retained some of this inter-millennial fervor, particularly in his emphasis upon spiritual perfection and his belief that this perfection was necessary and proper, because of man's relation to God. Perfection was an attribute of God which gave man this hope.

Not only were orthodox theologians wrong about the nature of God and man, they were also wrong about the nature of creation. Dissecting their view of creation, James found it incompatible with his conception of an active, creative God. James was especially concerned with the dilemma into which Puritan thought had gotten. From the start the Puritans had maintained that Adam's evil, accruing to all men, was not caused by natural desire but by will. This made the sin more heinous. Adam, however, derived his will from God. It must follow then that God willed evil into the world. If evil inheres in man, it must come from God.[30] God, in taking credit for good, also had to take responsibility for evil.

James attacked both ideas, that creation had come about through God's will and that man's nature was sinful. James maintained that the Old Theology (all that had preceded him) started with God voluntarily creating through the will. This view was wrong, for it created two problems which James assumed did not exist. In the first place the idea that God created through the fiat of His will implied that God was imperfect and finite, that God had to employ extraordinary measures to create, an action that James believed involuntary.[31] Interpreting creation as a spontane-

---

[29] Trowbridge, *Swedenborg*, pp. 117-18.

[30] Ralph Barton Perry, *Puritanism and Democracy* (New York: Vanguard, 1944), p. 388.

[31] Henry James, *Lectures and Miscellanies*, pp. 152-55.

ous action, James thought that God created because He could not help Himself, creative activity being a function of His total personality. The use of will implied that creative activity was foreign to God except through the instrumentality of this outside agent. James's position here was similar to those religious thinkers who minimized the power of God in order to emphasize His goodness and truth. God was restricted by His own nature, rather than omnipotent through His will. James preferred to think that God was more concerned with mercy than power.

In his second objection to the traditional view of God, James postulated that will, even as an attribute of God, was fickle. If men were entirely dependent upon God's will, they would be miserably insecure.[32] And insecurity was an intolerable quality in man's relationship with God, for insecurity was conducive to hate and not to love. According to James, the orthodox view of creation misrepresented the situation badly. He had to posit a creation which was worthy of a creative, perfect God and which was conducive to man's security.

Not only had the orthodox conception of creation given wrong implications, but it also had produced unsatisfactory results. If man, as a result of creation, was imperfect and tinged with original sin, creation had been a failure.[33] Since religious thought based on imperfect creation had to end with man's being radically changed, the destiny of man was to be treated and medicated until he was fit for heaven. All of man's life had to be devoted to remedying the original error of creation. By a single pragmatic test creation had failed, since it did not create a perfect man or even hint at the possibility of perfection. Instead, man had to gain perfection through further intervention by God. Given this erroneous view of creation, there was no possibility that man, created with a constitutional disability, had the capacity to achieve perfection.

The great majority of religious thinkers, James maintained, had made the mistake of assuming that creation was an historical occurrence, that is, limited by space and time. If space and time were subjective, existing only in man's mind, and if creation was limited to history, creation can be said not to have existed prior to the beginning of time and space. Creation was a function of God and existed prior to the subjective experience of space and time, and a view that held that creation was primarily

[32] *Ibid.,* pp. 154-55.
[33] *Ibid.,* pp. 292-93.

historical was untenable unless it also assumed that space and time co-existed with God. This would be absurd since it would make God finite.[34] James stated that creation either had to be a function of God or else God was finite. Since creation was a property of God, it took on most of the qualities of God. Creation was, therefore, infinite, perfect, and active, as God and creation could not be separated.

In order to allow man and God to remain on the friendliest of terms, James discarded the concept of an absolute creation, occurring in space and time, and substituted one that emphasized the spiritual nature of the action, in place of the material nature. God's primary creation consisted of men and not material objects; hence God created when He contributed Himself to man.[35] When man received goodness and truth, he was the true creature of a creative God.

The relation of God to man was not an absolute one. James considered an absolute relationship involving factors of space and time as unthinkable, since this would mean that God was subject to nature like an animal and was related to man by space and time. God should be nearer to man than to the horse; He must be in man. Man ought to claim an affinity to God more intimate than that common to animals and himself. To do this, the world of space and time must be regarded as a secondary product of the act of creation and not as the primary one. The real world was compared to the realm of "affection and thought," which was common only to God and man.[36] This spiritual creation, as James chose to call it, was the basis of James's religious thought.

A psychologist might have had a field day with James's constant reiteration that the real world was not the physical one.

> The finite world, the world of nature, in which time and space are fixed, is doubtless of indispensable use to embody this interior world, and afford it conscious development; but it is not the true world any more than a man's body is the true man. One physical perfection may be greatly impaired: he may lose his arms and his legs, and grow blind and deaf in addition. You would not thereupon say that he had lost his manhood.[37]

Henry James had lost one of his legs in a childhood accident. How far could one go in attributing some of his subsequent ideas, including the statement of the unreality of the physical world, to

[34] *Ibid.,* p. 321.
[35] Henry James, *The Nature of Evil,* pp. 292-93.
[36] *Ibid.,* pp. 297-98.
[37] *Ibid.,* p. 298.

this loss? It would be difficult and beyond the scope of this study, but it is interesting to speculate upon, nonetheless.

Spiritual creation was only perfect, however, when it resulted in true creatures. A true creature, in turn, would be independent; he would conceive of no creator except himself.[38] Yet James believed this to be impossible since God created and upheld men. The contradictory requirements of creation resulted in men assuming that they were not created by God while at the same time displaying God's handiwork.[39] The only true creature who could reconcile those contradictions was man; man originally thinks he is independent and then realizes he is dependent upon God. The independence of man was an illusion.

The necessity of a perfect result of creation caused certain problems; man must be perfect or else he could have come only from an imperfect God.[40] It was then necessary that man should share the attributes of God, one of which was freedom. How could a creator impart freedom to man when "there is not and cannot be a fibre of real or essential freedom in man, because he is essentially, and immutably a creature, deriving all of his *living* or *being* power from another than himself every moment, and *a fortiori* of course all his affection, thought and action?"[41] This was one of the most difficult problems James faced. The Creator was bound to conceal Himself from the creature in order that the creature might have freedom of action, yet that creature was nothing without God.[42] James reconciled these difficulties in his own unique way.

Since the only adequate form for revealing divine life is man, and since man requires freedom of action to emulate God, the Creator gave man the appearance of living in himself.[43] By this method man seems free and independent. But man is not free, not by any means; he has only the illusion of freedom. It is by the fiction of seeming independent that James reconciles the conflicting necessities of God's overwhelming presence and man's true representation of God. If James's explanation is accepted on face value, the problem is solved. Other religious thinkers have used equivalent devices, so James may be justified in so doing. The

[38] William James, p. 237.
[39] Henry James, *The Secret of Swedenborg*, p. 17.
[40] Henry James, *Lectures and Miscellanies*, p. 386.
[41] William James, p. 352.
[42] Henry James, *The Secret of Swedenborg*, pp. 44-45.
[43] Henry James, *The Church of Christ Not an Ecclesiasticism*, 2nd ed. (London: Walton and Mitchell, 1856), pp. 56-57.

freedom of man was as important to James as it was to the Unitarians and Transcendentalists, but the power of God was also as essential as it was to the Calvinists. It is interesting to speculate upon which James would have chosen had he been forced to take one or the other.

Not only was man's freedom desirable for the sake of mir-roring God's freedom, but also because it had an important de-rivative function. The gift of freedom from God was preliminary or mediatorial rather than final, as God did not intend to ex-press His indifference to the spiritual destiny of man. Man pos-sessed freedom only in order that he might become spiritually elevated to image divine perfection. This end was the use for which freedom existed, for only if man were free could he com-bine his natural self with the divine to merge into the ideal humanity.[44]

James had placed God in an almost intolerable position, in that God, although He had taken up residence in man, was forced to erase Himself from man's consciousness. God, says James, could not be compared to an artist, for an artist demands credit for his work above all other considerations. Also, the artist welcomed difficulties only as they afforded opportunity to expand his work by overcoming them, while God passively submitted to all sorts of evil possibilities from which only man could release Him.[45] This was the ultimate expression of the infinite love of God, the subjection of God to all the stupidity and evil that man might do in order that man may have freedom of choice.[46]

Perfect, infinite love came from God and was the keynote of His relation with man. This love asked nothing for itself; in fact, its concern was primarily with the best way to communicate itself to man.[47] More perfect love could not be imagined than that God should enter into and partake of man's nature in order to allow human nature to become equal with God. James pos-sessed a natural animosity to the God he inherited from his youthful education about God; only the concept of God humbling Himself to enter man filled James with devout love.[48] James admitted frankly that only a God actively concerned with the ex-pression of love to man was any kind of God at all. Julia Ward Howe reported that James once remarked to her that "God is

[44] Henry James, *The Nature of Evil*, pp. 101-02.
[45] William James, pp. 338-39.
[46] *Ibid.*, p. 34.
[47] Henry James, *The Secret of Swedenborg*, p. 41.
[48] Henry James, *Substance and Shadow*, p. 22.

working all the time in his shirt-sleeves with all His might."[49] Participating actively in the less attractive side of man's life, God was a workaday deity.

Risks were to be expected in spiritual creation, where man was given the illusion of freedom; man might accept this illusion as absolute freedom. One of the ways in which this kind of mistake manifested itself was the belief of some men that physical existence was identical with real being. An assumption like this led to the view that God had not created man and had no responsibility or concern for man.[50] Independence quite possibly could have exactly the opposite effect on man than was intended, with man growing increasingly self-reliant. God, however, took this calculated risk.

The device designed to assure man of his self-sufficiency was nature. The fact that God was all and man nothing, Swedenborg and James agreed, required some temporary meeting ground where the opposites could meet.[51] Nature was the key to the question of how man could seem free; man's own physical existence showed him that he was independent from other individuals.

Nature, to James, was the physical universe, excluding man. Man was the only creature who was in nature but not of it. Lacking positive value, nature (or "uncreation," as James called it) had the negative function of demonstrating to man what would happen if he had only physical existence.[52] This, of course, was death.

The immanence of God was restricted to man; and only man was immanent in nature. Just as man reflected God, so did nature reflect man. Nature had another function in thus representing man. Man's affections and thoughts were portrayed in the natural world; the lion and other animals correspond to attributes of man.[53] James considered that each animal had a peculiar and outstanding characteristic — ferocity, cunning, etc. — which was also contained in man in varying degrees. Subordinate to the use for which it was planned, physical existence gave apparent being to man and reflected his thought and direction.

Revealing and confirming the universe of time and space, man's

---

[49] Julia Ward Howe, *Reminiscences* (Boston: Houghton Mifflin, 1900), p. 323.
[50] William James, p. 209.
[51] *Ibid.*, p. 30.
[52] *Ibid.*, p. 213.
[53] James, as quoted in Warren, p. 196.

senses were to be considered as doors opening into man and not
out into nature. Thus the senses, the instruments by which man
confirmed his physical existence, belonged to nature or the world
of space or time.[54] However, man was a part of nature; that fact
he could not escape. But since physical existence was only temporary, man ought to concentrate upon spiritual existence. In spite of
being secondary, natural existence was important; this was never
denied, for physical appearance gave God phenomenality.[55] Natural man and spiritual God had a reciprocal arrangement, both
being necessary to the other.

Nature, while only a reflection of man's thought and affection,
was the meeting ground between man and God and was necessary only as it individualized man and allowed him, in turn, to
be useful to God. One notes that James always alludes to this
meeting as taking place between finite and infinite mind. This
was not accidental, for James believed that a synonym for divine
wisdom was created nature, that divine wisdom was divine love
in creaturely form.[56] The mental nature of creation, of man and
God, was important to James, as is illustrated by his equation
of human nature and mind. The spiritual world existed only in
the mind, which surmounted space and time.[57]

God, however, did not create individual minds or natures; He
created one mind, one nature, as He imparted Himself. Created
nature meant the unity common to all men, who partook equally
of universal human nature or mind.[58] Only physical existence
separated one man from another, for the natural world created
the impression that man's needs and desires were antagonistic.
God could have permitted nature to make the common unity of
man more evident, but this would have infringed upon man's
freedom to discover the truth for himself; therefore, it was not
done. The common stamp of brotherhood was one of the lessons
man had to learn for himself. Differences between men were the
same as the difference between heaven and hell, a contrasting
relationship to God, "or to the life of God in nature, which is
a life of perfect freedom or spontaneity";[59] but James always re-

[54] Henry James, *Lectures and Miscellanies*, p. 329.
[55] Henry James, *The Secret of Swedenborg*, pp. 28-29.
[56] *Ibid.*, p. 42.
[57] Henry James, *Christianity the Logic of Creation* (New York: D.
Appleton, 1857), p. 8.
[58] Henry James, *Society the Redeemed Form of Man* (Boston: Houghton,
Osgood, 1879), p. 280.
[59] William James, p. 85.

tained the fundamental axiom that even the lowest of men were given being by God.[60]

Creation, as viewed by the popular mind, was an event in time and space. James denied this and emphasized instead the essential flux in the process of creation. One of the reasons James rejected the traditional view of creation was that it was imperfect; yet his view also was imperfect, as it gave man supposed freedom and individuality while hiding God's power and man's common unity. If this became permanent, it would also be discreditable to God.[61] Creation becomes perfect only when the creator and the creature are reconciled; therefore the reverse of creation is redemption. Redemption completed the work begun by creation and thus perfected creation. Redemption and creation could be understood best in terms of each other, as they were concerned with the same process.[62]

One of the most difficult problems in James's theology was the problem of evil. What started Adam on the path to evil? James had attacked orthodox theology for implying that God created evil. In the first place James denied that Adam fell; instead he maintained that what was commonly considered the fall was actually an elevation. Adam in his undefiled state in Eden was symbolic of man in a completely physical state. Since the difference between man and animals was a sense of sin, man in a physical state approximated a brute.[63] Adam was not forbidden to eat of the tree of knowledge; God merely assured man that death would result if he did, which, in fact, occurred, since man discovered a personal, individual good. Finite good could only lead to infinite perplexity, since it was the property of man and not of God.[64]

Eve had a regenerative influence upon Adam, starting him on the path to true manhood. By giving him the fruit of the tree to eat, Eve allowed Adam to gain personal consciousness, the first step toward regeneration.[65] The fall did not mean that man went from good to evil;[66] it merely meant that man gained enough confidence to choose between good and evil, without leaving this to God.[67] One notes two distinguishing features about Adam's

---

60 *Ibid.,* p. 240.
61 *Ibid.,* p. 30.
62 Henry James, *The Church of Christ Not an Ecclesiasticism,* p. 60.
63 Henry James, *The Nature of Evil,* p. 26.
64 William James, pp. 224-25.
65 *Ibid.*
66 Henry James, *The Nature of Evil,* p. 129.
67 William James, p. 356.

fall. The first is that Adam's fall and the original product of spiritual creation are identical, as both imply man's freedom and growing selfhood. The second was the value James placed upon the moral life, where man personally chooses good or evil. This may appear strange coming from a man with a strong reputation for antinomianism, but James never pretended that the purely physical life was equal or superior to the moral life. For the moral life was the essence of human life, the one that distinguished men from each other as individuals.[68] The moral life became evil only when it obscured the spiritual life.

The presence of sin and evil in James's world demanded an explanation. How was sin to be reconciled with the perfection of God?[69] James knew that the visible evidence for evil convinced many people of its reality. This outward evidence was less important for James than the philosophical explanation of the existence of evil. The dilemma was a very real one, since James denied that evil could come from God. If it came from the devil (whom James defined collectively as "the whole mass of human kind in whom either the love of the world or the love of self predominates"),[70] however, either God had allowed evil to come into the world from some other source on the assumption that it could not injure man or else He lacked the power to prevent the introduction of evil.[71] The latter solution denied God's omnipotence, so James rejected it in favor of the view that evil was harmless.

In order to understand evil better, James divided it into its component parts — physical, moral, and spiritual.[72] Physical evil was that which was contrary to man's sense of right — stealing, murder, or the desire to do these things. Spiritual evil was what one was; this inhered in man despite anything he did. Since James considered spiritual evil more dangerous than physical, it was the one with which he was more concerned.

What was spiritual sin or evil? One might very easily assume that it was the original sin of the Calvinists. But James categorically denied this. Spiritual evil was synonymous with selfhood or self-sufficiency.[73] The instrument that discovered spiritual sin was

---

[68] Henry James, "Faith and Science," *North American Review,* CI (1865), p. 375.

[69] Henry James, *The Nature of Evil,* p. 42.

[70] Henry James, *Society the Redeemed Form of Man,* p. 199.

[71] Henry James, "Socialism and Civilization," in *Moralism and Christianity,* p. 166.

[72] Henry James, *The Nature of Evil,* pp. 70-71.

[73] William James, p. 51.

the conscience,[74] which informed man that it was impossible for
him to achieve good, as only God could do that. The real evil
against which conscience fought was spiritual evil, the attribution
of good to man's own effort instead of to God.

Since the idea of selfhood was produced by creation and was
designed to allow man freedom, are we to assume that God, in
producing selfhood, produced evil? James said no, and the reason
he used was that God had merely created man and become in-
conspicuous. Man, at his inception, was a neutral in the complete
sense of the word. Two forces, however, operated upon man. One
of these was from God, the force of universal humanity; and the
other was from the devil, the force of selfhood. Everything contributing to the assumption that man was a free agent, separate
and antagonistic to other men, was a source of evil, while, conversely, everything contributing to the assumption of a common
humanity was a force for good. From this original equality of
forces man must choose, placing himself in heaven or in hell. The
difference between a native of heaven and a native of hell is that
"the latter was always cherishing an unsubdued selfhood, or pride
of character; the former being always more or less cultivated out
of it."[75] One of the most difficult points to understand in James
is why, given an equilibrium of forces, man invariably chose
evil, as James assumed? One must conclude either that there was
no true equilibrium or that God had planned it this way.

James's entire treatment of the problem of evil seems unsatisfactory. It would seem that God, by positing a physical world that
gives man an illusion of freedom, caused selfhood or evil just as
surely as if he directly created it. Again, James changed his views
on evil from time to time, now emphasizing its reality, now denying it.

The real error, according to James, was the assumption that man
was free and independent. When men disabused themselves of this
impression, evil disappeared. If man recognized that good and
evil were not a part of him but only a product of the forces sur-
rounding him, he could confess his sins, the main one being his
mistake in thinking he had independence.[76] The other sins, physical
and moral, were unimportant, since they corrected themselves.[77]
James believed that these evils received their own rewards here

[74] Henry James, *The Nature of Evil*, p. 77.
[75] William James, pp. 82-83.
[76] Henry James, *Lectures and Miscellanies*, p. 413.
[77] Henry James, *Substance and Shadow*, p. 222.

on earth, and that evil experience was good for man. The suffering that men undergo was "invariably sanatory, and ends in
peace."[78] James thought that no man suffered for one hour without reaping infinite benefit. If men were good, pain, both physical
and moral, purified the soul; if they were bad, pain restrained
them from further wickedness.[79] Evil, like nature, was educative,
transitory, and dangerous only as man grew to love and gain
pleasure from it. One wonders how much James's own childhood
suffering shaped his faith.

Since moral and physical evil were educative and did not
separate man from God, they did not disturb God. The only true
sin that man could commit was to separate himself from God; he
could not sin through moral or physical evil.[80] God did not concern
Himself, therefore, with man's poverty, disease, or crime, since
these were not His real enemies. Man's wealth, health, and morality were God's most dangerous enemies, as these qualities caused
man to overvalue his own strength and to reenforce his selfhood.[81] If man really had become contaminated by the evil he
did, as popular opinion held, he could not voluntarily dissociate
himself from it by confession.[82] Only the fact that evil did not
touch men enabled God to hate evil in man without hating man.
Also, since God created man and proceeded to uphold him, it
would be "devilish" for Him to hate man for anything he had
done.[83] If God was responsible for man's acts, these acts could not
harm man. James emphasized this point repeatedly; God does not
hate the sin of man but only his self-righteousness,[84] since this
separated God and man.

How could a man lose his selfhood and gain salvation? In
James's childhood most Protestants assumed that all men deserved
God's censure, regardless of their works, and that salvation was
entirely derived from God's grace. But in practice this concept
became somewhat perverted by the idea that perhaps the outward
signs of regeneration were the important determinants of a saintly
man. Morality came to distinguish saint from sinner. As a boy,
James had learned that "being good consisted of attending family

---

[78] Henry James, *The Nature of Evil*, p. 216.
[79] *Ibid.*
[80] Henry James, as quoted in F. O. Matthiessen, *The James Family*
(New York: Alfred A. Knopf, 1947), p. 52.
[81] Henry James, *Substance and Shadow*, p. 222.
[82] Henry James, *Lectures and Miscellanies*, p. 203.
[83] William James, p. 219.
[84] Henry James, *Lectures and Miscellanies*, p. 209.

prayers and loving one's relations and bestowing charity upon the needy poor about one."[85] James reacted against this view by presenting his own plan of salvation. All a man had to do to be saved was to confess himself nothing and to believe that the God which was inside of him was all.[86] This was not a startling theological doctrine; Luther would certainly have accepted it.

Unlike either Luther or Calvin, however, James remained somewhat uncertain as to just who would be saved. Sometimes James indicated that salvation belonged only to those who believed as he did, that man was nothing and God was all.[87] On the other hand, James demanded a perfect Creator and a perfect creation, which would presuppose that there would be an economy of salvation whereby every man would be saved.[88] James never completely reconciled these two views in a satisfactory manner.

Perhaps one of the reasons for this confusion was James's unique view of heaven and hell. These were not objective realities for James; rather they were relative and subjective.[89] Signifying mental states primarily, heaven and hell presented the two positions of man relative to God. A devil supposed himself independent from God, while an angel recognized his dependence upon God. If heaven and hell were absolutes, the devil would actually be independent; as it was, both angels and devils were supported by God. Supposedly then, one remained in hell until he understood the truth, at which time he ascended into heaven, despite his age or whether alive or dead. Heaven and hell, being only descriptive of states of men, were transitory. In the end these temporary states will vanish in the true immortality of the race, frustrating any personal hopes of salvation or fears of damnation.[90] One notes that man could be happy and lead a good life whether he was in heaven or hell.

Heaven and hell were attitudes which man possessed and which man could choose freely. If he preferred to remain in hell, assuming that he was independent, this was acceptable, and man need not suffer thereby. On the other hand man entered heaven of his own free will also. Man could not be forced into either heaven or hell, since force would negate the freedom which God tried to

85 Austin Warren, pp. 6-7.
86 Henry James, *Lectures and Miscellanies*, p. 170.
87 Henry James, *The Nature of Evil*, p. 196.
88 Henry James, *Shadow and Substance*, p. 73.
89 William James, p. 136.
90 Henry James, *Society the Redeemed Form of Man*, pp. 252-53.

give men.[91] Man went to heaven and hell as he willed, so these were as subjective as will itself.

Personal salvation, according to James, was unimportant. In his autobiography, written under the pseudonym of Stephen Dewhurst, he proclaimed his disinterest in any question of personal salvation or damnation, since God was adequate for either expedient.[92] The salvation which concerned James the most was the salvation of universal man rather than personal man. In fact, the notion of salvation smacked too much of personal ambitions for James to stomach: "There is no gospel of universal salvation for in the nature of things that event is contingent upon human will; but the gospel tells of universal redemption and consequent at-one-ment."[93]

Since, then, redemption reflected more glory upon God than did salvation, James preferred to speak of it. The two, redemption and salvation, were separate and not to be confused. Even in the early church, the Apostles had made this distinction. Salvation was an event in the future which they hoped would occur because of the act of redemption effected by Christ.[94] The great redemptive work of Christ was to redeem the entire human race.

Leading men back into union with God, redemption supplemented the original, separative work of creation. It was the inward or spiritual being of creation designed to invest man with divine good.[95] In this sense redemption, as conceived by both James and Swedenborg, was more glorious than creation;[96] for redemption completed the positive phase of creation which had the negative task of separating God and man. Redemption added a new factor to the nature of both God and man, for God and man unified to produce the final God, divine-natural humanity.

The product of redemption was human society in its perfected form.[97] Resulting from the union of the divine and the natural, redemption, like salvation, resulted partially from man's puny contributions. God must allow man to work out his redemption with the resources He provided, primarily by created consciousness. God, again, did not intervene from the outside to produce the desired result;[98] redemption comes finally from man's experience.

---

[91] Henry James, *The Nature of Evil,* p. 262.
[92] William James, p. 130.
[93] Henry James, *The Nature of Evil,* p. 198.
[94] *Ibid.,* pp. 161-62.
[95] William James, p. 335.
[96] *Ibid.,* p. 31.
[97] Henry James, *The Church of Christ Not an Ecclesiasticism,* p. 98.
[98] William James, p. 32.

The sole purpose of social life, moral law, and education was to redeem the race of man. Supreme love could unite with self-love only as man educated and developed the social instincts by refraining from anti-social behavior.[99] After society was redeemed, man took on a characteristic regenerate form which was a social one. The outstanding trait of this social form was the renunciation of personal pride in favor of pride in the total race of man.[100]

A question that must invariably rise was how man discovered the nature of God in order to gain salvation and promote redemption? From what source could man learn to know himself and his relation to God? Knowledge was, after all, the necessary first step toward redemption, for only after man obtained a true picture of himself could he renounce his exclusive love of self and substitute love for his neighbor.[101] However, another problem also presented itself. How could man secure the idea that he was insufficient in himself, if God had been as careful as James indicated in hiding Himself?

Revelation was the key to knowledge of spiritual existence, as it operated within the scope of nature. Divine truth, by its very characteristics, could not be transmitted to man in its pure form, since that would be overwhelming. Revelation presented divine truth veiled over to accommodate man's nascent intelligence.[102] Since the world of sense had given man his conception of individuality, it could never inform him of his spiritual destiny. Revelation had two qualities for James: first, it was more than simple empirical fact, since the world of sense furnished that; second, it did not contradict science, which organized sense data into meaningful patterns.[103]

Revelation, for James, was comprehended by reason. As man advanced out of his race infancy, he came to live by reason, "an appreciation of things according to their substance."[104] James concluded that reason operated along the lines of correspondence. He echoed Emerson in admiring Swedenborg for such an important insight. Reason, operating on data furnished by the senses,

99 Henry James, *Society the Redeemed Form of Man,* p. 268.

100 *Ibid.,* p. 325.

101 Henry James, "The Reconciliation of Man Individual with Man Universal," *The Index,* VII (1867), 52.

102 Henry James, "Faith and Science," *The North American Review,* CI (1865), 376-77.

103 Henry James, *The Secret of Swedenborg,* p. 67.

104 Henry James, "Works of Sir William Hamilton," *Putnam's Monthly,* II (1853), 472-73.

was superior to the dictates of sense but could never alter them.[105] Since revelation was aimed at the spiritual side of man and could not be understood naturally, natural symbols visible to the senses had a much deeper meaning than their surface ones. The meanings of these natural symbols were transmitted through history, so that history constituted one of the main educative agents for men.[106]

James could not demonstrate the accuracy of these natural symbols, for they transcended his critical faculty and etched themselves upon his heart. As he said, "I am just as incapable of measuring in terms of the analytical intellect, or reducing the contrast of the true and the false, as I am of demonstrating to a blind man the pleasure of a gorgeous sunset, or reasoning a man without a palate into the savor of sugar."[107] With regard to the accuracy of revelation as with regard to the existence of God, James merely posited the necessity for faith. He could never have empirically proven that mother love symbolized God's love or that marriages on earth represented the union of natural and divine elements in a glorified society.

One would probably assume then that James was a believer in miracles. This assumption, however, would be correct only in a limited sense. James conceded the necessity of miracles for the spiritually naive man, since this sort of evidence was the only kind that a carnal mind could understand.[108] As for his own day, James noted the quarrel between the Unitarians and Transcendentalists over miracles and quite accurately described the difference as being over the mode of operation of God's power, since both groups admitted the power of God. They disagreed on whether God used His power in nature in individual cases or on all occasions. James stated flatly that the latter view was the one he preferred,[109] thus placing himself on the side of the Transcendentalists as against the Unitarians.

Miracles, as defined by James, were synonymous with revelation. Miracles could not violate man's sense impressions, nor could they destroy facts, as this was absurd. Even the Christian miracles had power only to shed light upon the "ordinary facts of experience."[110] James nowhere made a very clear distinction between the

---

[105] Henry James, *Substance and Shadow*, p. 313.

[106] Henry James, "Faith and Science," p. 376.

[107] Henry James, *Society the Redeemed Form of Man*, p. 114.

[108] *Ibid.*, p. 291.

[109] Henry James, Review of Lecky's *History of the Rise and Influence of the Spirit of Rationalism in Europe*, *Atlantic Monthly*, XVII (1866), 249-250.

[110] William James, p. 242.

two ideas of revelation and miracle, although he discounted miracles while insisting upon the necessity of revelation. Perhaps he favored revelation for its continuous flow of illumination instead of the intermittent light miracles were supposed to give.

For James, then, man was created and given selfhood, and by revelation gained knowledge that led him to salvation. Salvation could be effected by anyone who recognized his own insufficiency and allowed himself to be taken over by God; and redemption was progressing inevitably through the world. William James, an astute critic of his father, cannily laid a finger on the weakness of James's theology: "I confess . . . that I am myself unable to see any radical and essential necessity for the mission of Christ in his scheme of the universe."[111] The system was complete and perfect without Christ; James had a religion, but was it Christian?

From his early years, however, James had an emotional need for Christ. As he himself indicated, his early conception of the nature of God was that He was a stern disciplinarian, fearfully intolerant toward sin and sinners. The only hope sustaining James, as he was incapable of accepting any theological dogma as true, was mercy through Christ's atonement.[112] James retained an emotional need for an intercessor all his life, so a place was made for Christ in his system of redemption.

In a statement of faith James presented a creed that would have been sympathetically received by almost any religious traditionalist:

> I hold (perhaps more strenuously than you can at present imagine) that Christ was conceived of the Holy Ghost, that he was born of a virgin, that he lived a life of helpless humiliation and infamy in the eyes of most reputable people of his age and nation, while at the same time he became inwardly united with the Divine spirit to such a degree as at length to grow exanimate on his finite or maternal side, and find his literal flesh and blood becoming vivified by the infinite love.[113]

James did not agree that Christ died in order to placate divine wrath, for this view made God a savage with a terrible, inhuman streak.[114] Christ had come to purify human nature, but the need for purification was due to man's self-instituted obstacles to God and not to God-instituted ones. Man owed no debt of blood to

---

111 *Ibid.,* pp. 106-07.
112 Matthiessen, *The James Family,* pp. 24-25.
113 Henry James, *Christianity the Logic of Creation,* p. 193.
114 Henry James, *Substance and Shadow,* p. 165.

God and no difference existed between them, since both were composed of the same substance.

James's main concern, however, was to place the recorded facts of Christ's life, which he believed implicitly, within a symbolic framework. James wished to know what Christ's death meant in the light of revelation, as Christ's historic value was secondary when compared to this philosophic one.[115] The older theological views had concentrated too much upon the historic importance of Jesus; they had supposed that Jesus had actually changed God's nature, softening Him and making Him more magnanimous and merciful. If Christ had not done this, God would have not been perfect.[116] James, holding as he did to the idea of a God perfect in Himself, rejected this view. Christ was only the symbol that revealed God's plan for the world, the victory of good over evil in the human mind.[117] But if the only function of Christ was to reveal God's plan for the world, which plan was revealed by other agents, William James was right in denying Christ's necessity in his father's universe.

James, however, had conceived of another purpose for Jesus in the process of redemption. Jesus had actually brought about redemption, said James, and the key by which He did so was His assumption of human nature, thus subjecting God to man.[118] But this too is unsatisfactory, since if this was the extent of Jesus' contribution, He was synonymous with creation. Does James mean to imply that creation took place only with the coming of Christ? A considerable amount of evidence supports this interpretation.

Perhaps the best way to attack the problem would be to consider James's view of the accomplishments of Christ, relative to His position in an economy of salvation. In the first place Christ possessed very little moral or personal force, so little, in fact, that He was dependent upon a few poor women for the necessities of life. This, according to James, might well argue a much larger amount of spiritual manhood than anyone else had.[119] Not only was Christ preoccupied with spiritual force rather than with material needs, but He assumed all the evils and temptations of the flesh. Experiencing man's nature gave Christ an intimate feeling for human weakness and enabled Him to subject the evil or

---

[115] Henry James, *Lectures and Miscellanies,* p. 161.

[116] *Ibid.,* p. 158.

[117] Henry James, *The Church of Christ Not an Ecclesiasticism,* p. 83.

[118] Henry James, *The Nature of Evil,* p. 5.

[119] Henry James, Review of Foster's translation of *The True Christian Religion, Atlantic Monthly,* XXIII (1869), 766-67.

infernal principle and "practically to recreate or regenerate human nature."[120]

The subjection of evil to good, in James's opinion, marked the difference between personal salvation and universal redemption. One was saved personally by renouncing self and relying upon God. Salvation was accomplished by a simple act of will in which evil was removed but not converted. In redemption, on the other hand, evil was incorporated into good. Christ's economy made use of evil, subject as it was, to further the aims of an evolving perfection. (The notion of an evolving perfection is, of course, somewhat difficult to defend, given the popular definition of perfection as a stable rather than a flexible entity.) As Christ united human nature with divine nature, His very bones and flesh became glorified.[121] Man's natural nature with its evil and good became divine.

James illustrated the difference between salvation and redemption as partaking of the same qualities as the differences separating angels and Christ. One might assume that both angels and Christ would share the same substance, God, and, therefore, be equal. James, however, maintained that there was a considerable difference between what he called the regenerate nature of man, typified by angels, and the glorified nature of man, typified by Christ. Angels were purified of self; Christ combined self into a union with God.[122] One difficulty with this distinction is that the assumption here is that self is a tangible contribution to the nature of God, providing a much higher estimate of self than James had previously allowed.

James further distinguished the two stages of man by calling Christ's contribution, natural regeneration, as opposed to God's spiritual regeneration. Christ could not deliver a man from hell into heaven, but He could regenerate the entire human race. Natural regeneration meant an emphasis upon the common unity of all men. Before Christ's life, man was separated from God and desired union with God only out of selfish, personal motives; after this event, selfhood could be used as a direct route to God instead of a block to it.[123]

Consequently, the outstanding result of Christ's sacrifice was the extended freedom of man. Christ's goal was to free men from government, priesthoods, and "institutions of all sorts which arro-

---

[120] Henry James, *The Nature of Evil*, p. 327.
[121] Henry James, *Society the Redeemed Form of Man*, pp. 184-85.
[122] Henry James, *Christianity the Logic of Creation*, p. 22.
[123] Henry James, *The Nature of Evil*, pp. 328-29.

gated to themselves the right of controlling human action."[124] The purpose of Christ had been accomplished, for the spiritual freedom which man had forfeited in Adam was now restored in the second Adam, Christ. Men so disposed might go to heaven without "gratuitous embarrassment," and men with infernal inclinations might pursue them "without coercion."[125] Those in hell were not separated from God but, like those in heaven, were an integral part of Him.[126]

Thus the old ecclesiastical reference to the resurrection of man was wrong when taken in the literal sense, since it confused man with his physical constitution.[127] True immortality would not be a permanent residence in heaven or hell, but would rather be a loss of personal haughtiness in a feeling of equality with the rest of mankind.[128] A new social principle had resulted, one which combined universal love with self-love. "Universal love alone, or self-love alone, would alike defeat society; the one because it would render its subject indifferent to any special fellowship, the other because it would render him averse to all fellowship."[129]

God could be conceived of as a great man, combining internal or spiritual elements, love and wisdom, with natural ones, appetite and passions.[130] God was roughly equivalent to humanity or the spirit of society, for they combined the same elements and had the same goal, a sense of equality and freedom. God, so evolved, becomes apparent when the entire human race finally realizes that there is no difference between men, good or evil, insofar as their spiritual worth is concerned.

The union of God with man was inevitable, since it was a concomitant of God and not of man; man could only hinder that progress by committing sins and obscuring the facts of human fellowship.[131] A true creature of God was, then, not the moral or the immoral man, but the humble man who knows that the difference between himself and his neighbor is not a product of his own efforts.[132] Recognition of this important fact was implicit in the education James gave his children, "the moral of all of which

124 Henry James, *Lectures and Miscellanies,* p. 221.
125 Henry James, *The Nature of Evil,* p. 189.
126 William James, p. 285.
127 Henry James, *The Nature of Evil,* pp. 295-96.
128 Henry James, "Spiritualism New and Old," *Atlantic Monthly,* XXIX (1872), 360.
129 Henry James, "Swedenborg as a Theologian," p. 207.
130 Henry James, *Society the Redeemed Form of Man,* p. 176.
131 *Ibid.,* pp. 10-11.
132 Henry James, *The Nature of Evil,* p. 224.

education," said Henry James, Jr., "was that we need never fear not to be good enough, if we were only social enough: a splendid meaning indeed being attached to the latter term."[133]

In the end all will be redeemed by natural redemption, since all will be needed in the good society. Personal salvation will become unimportant for the individual as he participates in society. However, several problems are brought to mind by James's ideas. The progression James indicated went from the divine, which was perfect and active, to the natural man, who was nothing in himself, to humanity, which combined the two in a more perfect form. The divine element furnished spiritual being, while the natural element furnished phenomenal being, which was spiritually nothing. How could nothing contribute to a perfect God in such a way as to effect an improvement? Again, how could man, evil in his selfhood, combine with the perfection of God and retain his selfhood? For James the answer was Christ, who spanned the distance between God and man. This was not a logical, philosophical answer; it was a religious one. In the final analysis James relied upon faith.

James saw society as the redeemed form of man. This view gave him pride in Christianity, which he thought was superior to other religions for this very reason. Christianity was also superior because it stimulated and educated man's intellectual strivings toward God. There was no literal or direct path to God, according to James, but an "exclusively mystical and living witness of the ineffable Divine name."[134] Paganism was characterized by the belief that God was a power above nature but nonetheless intimately connected with it,[135] while Christianity was the only religion in which God was portrayed incarnate in His creatures, and the only religion which revealed God in human conditions.[136] Christianity had given James his taste of life.

> When I am really living, when I am obeying the full tide of life which pours into me from the inward sphere, I lose my self-consciousness, I feel only my intense unity with all men, with all things that have life. . . . I feel only the profound and boundless unity which God makes between me and whatsoever else that lives and moves and has its being in Him.[137]

---

[133] Henry James, Jr., *A Small Boy and Others* (New York: Charles Scribner's Sons, 1913), p. 216.

[134] Henry James, "Spiritualism New and Old," p. 361.

[135] Henry James, *Lectures and Miscellanies*, p. 310.

[136] Henry James, *The Church of Christ Not an Ecclesiasticism*, p. 51.

[137] Henry James, *Lectures and Miscellanies*, p. 77.

Even the most casual observer must be struck by the very sophisticated, metaphysical philosophy-religion that James constructed. His cosmological attempt surely indicated a high degree of original thought and a large amount of imaginative effort. The ability to grasp James's thought presupposes a very subtle, discerning mind; and any attempt to fit him into any rigid theological system must, in my opinion, inevitably fail. There are, nonetheless, certain aspects of James's system that strike familiar chords in historic memory; and James, standing as he does at the end of a progressive theological change from Calvinism through Transcendentalism, reveals some of the characteristics of the preceding systems.

One way to conceive James's system is to visualize two concentric spheres. In the inner sphere, the unreal and transitory world, man is a product of creation operating by his own will, who must acknowledge himself as nothing in order to be personally saved. In the larger sphere God is real, man is strictly determined, and Christ combines the two so that all humanity, evil and good, coalesces with God. Two distinct levels exist. On one, man is an individual; on the other, man lives only as a part of the race nature. The connecting link between the two spheres is Christ, who converts the smaller into the larger one.

In the personal sphere the element that would seem to connect James with the Calvinist tradition was his belief in the reality of evil, which might loosely be compared with original sin, a concept that James attacked. James insisted that selfhood was bad and that all men shared in the stigma. In addition, God's power was all that sustained man and, through man, the world. Puritanism would support this view, for the sense that God was the only good and man the only evil was the main point of Puritan piety. Dependence upon God as the only hope for the cleansing of evil would not have seemed out of place to Jonathan Edwards.

Then James proceeded to go from a Calvinist sense of piety to a statement of God's nature that was quite similar to the Unitarian statement. God was not a trinity, except as He was an evolutionary, creative process. God, Christ, and Humanity were identical except that they were different stages in the evolutionary process. Man was thought to be a rational creature, determining truth through knowledge gained from revelation and tempered by reason, and placing himself in heaven by an act of will based upon this knowledge. Man, in this sense, was supremely free to determine his own destiny, although the method of achieving salvation varied considerably from the method of moralism.

Some elements of Transcendentalism too could be pointed

out in James. Man's ability to gain salvation was a tenet of Transcendentalism as well as of Unitarianism. Certainly the Puritans would violently disagree with the idea that men could not be forced into either heaven or hell. So far as revelation and miracles were concerned, James occupied a position near to the Transcendental one, for he insisted upon a continuous revelation of God. James, however, maintained that revelation and immanence occurred in a somewhat different sphere than nature. One could say, with some justice, that James started with a Puritan concept of piety and God and then proceeded to assume that the Unitarian and Transcendental concepts of man's freedom of action were correct.

Other ideas in James, however, are not to be found in the theological schools of his time. His concepts of Jesus might be said to approximate quite clearly the Unitarian, so far as His sacrifice was not propitiatory but exemplary. There the resemblance stopped, for James believed that Christ had incorporated evil in a new, suggestive synthesis, as shown by Christ's lack of moral force and His abundance of spiritual force. The Calvinists would have been disturbed, as would the Unitarians and Transcendentalists, with the assumption that followed in James's view, namely, that redemption was universal and that God's relation to the evil or good man was impersonal.

James's view of nature was unique, denying both God's immanence in it and its absolute existence. Nature, for James, reflected man and not God, showing man's fate rather than God's design. His idea of God was also a singularly personal one. The Puritans, inheriting some of the Old Testament ideas, believed that men should serve and worship God somewhat as if he were an oriental despot. The Unitarians were convinced that men would grow more like God as they grew more moral and free, and that men should regard God a great moral teacher and mentor. The Transcendentalists hoped for man's assimilation into the great Oversoul hinted at in nature. But James turned men into God by unifying their natures. If one could say that the Unitarians turned man into God, one might also be justified in saying that James did the same thing.

James used his philosophy or theology as a key to unlock the problems facing the society of his day. He consistently thought of social and political relationships in terms of the relations of God and man. The progress of society and the unity of human nature upon which his political and social theories were based were articles of faith for James. It is to these more detailed conclusions about the nature of the individual and society that we must turn next, allowing William James the last word on his father's theology.

> It had many and diffuse affinities. It was optimistic in one sense, pessimistic in another. Pantheistic, idealistic, hegelian are epithets that very naturally arise on the reader's lip to describe it; and yet some part there is of the connotation of each of these epithets that made my father violently refuse to submit to their imposition. The ordinary empirical ethics of evolutionary naturalism can find a perfect *permis de sejour* under the system's wings; and yet close alongside is an insistence on the need of the death of the natural man and of a supernatural redemption, more thorough-going than what we find in the most evangelical protestantism. Dualism, yet monism; antinomianism, yet restraint; atheism (as we might almost name it — that is, the swallowing up of God in humanity) as the last result of God's achievement — such are some of the first aspects of this at bottom very simple and harmonious view of the world.[138]

---

[138] William James, pp. 14-15.

Four

Nature of Man

One who has had any encounter at all with James's thought has every reason to expect that his conception of the nature of man would not be ordinary. He would not be disappointed, as James's view of man was unusual in many ways. Man was important enough to be the center of the theological system James had created. He was the unit by which the world was measured.

Man, as we have seen, was not being, but the form of being that God took.[1] One of man's major goals, from the beginning, was to indicate God, for "the object implies the subject; existence implies substance; error implies truth; difference implies identity; *and never the contrary.*"[2] Man furnished proof of God's existence and enabled God to fulfill His nature by being actively creative. Since man's life was to convey meaning, he was not allowed to create for selfish, personal reasons. Nothing about man was unimportant. The belief that everything in the material world had a distinct purpose and place was a belief James clung to always, almost with the fervor of a medieval Christian. Given the importance of every event and the high estimate of man, nowhere more than in man was every minute detail deserving of careful scrutiny.

One of the first and most obvious facts James discovered in his observations about the human race was its division into two sexes. This division was shared with the animal world, but it was the unusual nature of the division that intrigued James. James examined the difference between man and woman and compared it to the difference between the male and female in the animal

---

[1] Henry James, "A Scientific Statement of the Lord of Divine Man," *Massachusetts Quarterly Review,* III (1850), 52.

[2] Henry James, Review of Stirling's *Secret of Hegel, North American Review,* CII (1866), 275.

world. The results of this comparison proved, to James's satisfaction, that sexual differentiation in man was different in kind from that in animals.

"It is contrary to the analogy of nature that the female of any species should display so signal a contrast to the male as to amount to a genetic diversity, and yet this is the difference woman exhibits to man."[3] James went on to cite several historical examples of women, who, at first glance, seem to disprove him: Boadicea, Queen Elizabeth, Catherine of Russia, and "doubtless some of those Indian princesses, whose example Mr. Mill has recently invoked."[4] Calling such aggressive women female men, James denied that they changed his generalization. Women had a character and genius which was so different from men that they might be termed a new species instead of the female counterpart to man.

The distinguishing characteristics of women were easy to discover. Women were naturally inferior to men, for men were more passionate, more intellectual, and physically stronger. James took this as an axiom.[5] In addition, women were incapable of any great philanthropy, for a woman's nature was to love a man, and hence she could not love the race.[6] Since the impetus for the reformation of society could not come from women, they played an inferior role in nature and society. We see this general view displayed in a compliment he paid to the wife of E. L. Godkin:

> I have seen no one since I saw you in Ripton to be compared with you; no one whom I esteem so much, and whom I love so much; *women are generally such slips of things, with so little root in nature, as to inspire only frivolous attachments,* while your qualities justify the manliest (italics mine).[7]

Lest any suspicion fall at his door, James always hastened to make clear that woman's natural inferiority was not to be considered a handicap. As a matter of fact, man's natural attributes caused him great difficulty in attaining the spiritual life, and the fact that women had weaker natural attachments meant that they were also more spiritual.

Functioning as the great agent for the spiritualization of man,

---

[3] Henry James, "The Woman Thou Gavest Me," *Atlantic Monthly,* XXV (1870), 66.

[4] *Ibid.*

[5] Henry James, "Woman and the Woman's Movement," *Putnam's Monthly Magazine,* I (1853), 285.

[6] *Ibid.,* p. 281.

[7] Ogden Rollo, ed., *Life and Letters of Edwin Lawrence Godkin,* I (New York: Macmillan, 1902), pp. 170-71.

women socialized man by marrying him. This conversion of a private desire into a public one, a particular desire to a universal one, was the main function of women. The whole constellation of social organizations from the family on up to the nation was produced by the catalytic action of women. By submitting to the will of man and subtly changing him, women built a new world and aided in the redemption of man into a perfect social order.[8] This action was valuable for its own sake and also for the large amount of symbolic truth it gave to man.

A simple test of the progress of society toward its perfect form was then forthcoming. Since women were the "perfect flower" and "perfect fruit" of spiritual progress, the position of women in any society determined how far that society had advanced toward perfect fellowship.[9] The more elevated and esteemed women were — short of dominating men, of course; James looked askance at any matriarchy — the more one could hope for society.

In the end, however, the difference between the sexes was permanent:

> Man is not man, nor woman woman, primarily by virtue of their formal difference from each other, but by virtue of their spiritual or interior differences, the difference of their genius or temper of mind. And where this fundamental difference does not exist the outward difference is only transient. .The natural body in that case has only to be laid aside by its decease, for the spiritual one to assert its latent sexuality; so that probably many a woman who has lain down on this side Jordan in short-gown and petticoat, will wake up by sheer spiritual gravitation on the other side in corduroys and top-boots, and many a man who has lain down in coat and pantaloons, will similarly come to true self-consciousness in petticoats and curl-paper.[10]

James would not have been regarded as a radical in his society for holding these views about women. He might, in fact, have been attacked by the more radical supporters of women's rights for being too conservative; certainly such an attack would have been justified. Exactly why James thought as he did is hard to determine. I think that he was perfectly sincere in his statements about women and that he thought he was improving the status of women by putting them on a higher plane than man, doing them a favor which they richly deserved. Regardless of what James intended, the fact remains that he shared the tenets of nineteenth-century male

---

[8] William James, p. 262.

[9] Henry James, *Substance and Shadow,* p. 211.

[10] Henry James, "Woman and the Woman's Movement," p. 281.

society about women. The perfect fellowship which he talked about would not be an equal one, so far as women were concerned. Women had a place, but their place was a rather rigidly defined inferior one.

As we continue our consideration of James's theories we must always keep in mind that when James talks of man, he means exactly that. Women had a passive, subordinate position, even though it was a more spiritual one. James divided man's life into two traditional categories, the physical and the mental. Physical existence was not the whole of life but was a means by which man could achieve life; it enabled man to learn, know, choose, love, and believe.[11] The body allowed the individual to meet and unite with universal man in the true world of the spirit, which was the mind of collective man.

> The spiritual world, or the mind of man, is out of space and time; and all God's alleged spiritual judgments which were expressed or ultimated in the life of Christ, claim your and my bosom for their veritable ground or arena, quite as much as they do that of any one who dies before Christ.[12]

The problem was how best to go from the area of man's physical existence to that of his mental existence.

It is extremely difficult to discuss James's view of the nature of man, since James held that man has several natures. These natures are good in their place but must give way to a higher good. Only the final product, the highest nature, deserved to be called man. This is what James meant when he said that "no man was ever born man; and only and at most he becomes man."[13] The change or growth of man through various stages was a natural product of man's life; he must expand both physically and mentally until he reaches his true estate.

Man's life consisted of three stages, according to James. These stages were (1) the instinctual or animal stage, which is the stage of the child; (2) the voluntary or moral stage, which is the stage of the adult who does good to commend himself to God or refrains from evil out of fear of the wrath of God; and (3) the spontaneous or spiritual stage, which is the stage of the man who does good because he heartily loves it.[14] Each man ought

---

[11] Henry James, Review of the *Works* of Sir William Hamilton, *Putnam's Monthly,* II (1853), 475.

[12] Henry James, *Christianity the Logic of Creation,* p. 8.

[13] Henry James, "Spiritualism New and Old," *Atlantic Monthly,* XXIX (1872), 362.

[14] Henry James, *The Church of Christ Not an Ecclesiasticism,* p. 85.

to pass through all of these stages to the final one; until he does reach the final stage, he does not become a real man.

Another characteristic of man's individual existence was action. "What I do, that I am. . . . What characterizes me, what gives me individuality, or distinctive genius, is my action."[15] There were two reasons why men had to be active. The first was that man had to be active to reflect God, who was also active.[16] The second was that man had to be active in order to be able to return to God.[17] The very nature of God's program of creation and redemption demanded free movement on the part of man. Man had action within his physical, moral, and spiritual natures; this action ought to be free, undetermined action, since God so placed Himself that man was unaware of His power. Even action that moved man away from God might occur, since this was a risk that freedom entailed.

James declared that most of the current theologies did not allow freedom of action for man and hence impaired his religious life. Since life consisted of the passage of ideas into action, popular theology restricted freedom by forbidding man to attack the restrictions that were placed upon him by existing social institutions.[18]

However, James was not so naive as to suppose that man was not impelled or determined in some fashion. He merely held that man's action would be least determined in the final stage of his progress. In the natural stage of man's life, man's actions were motivated by physical necessity, hunger, thirst, the desire for survival. In his moral stage man was compelled to act by legal necessity. Legal pressure was exerted to force man to pay debts, economic and social, because society called this necessary. In man's spontaneous stage the external compulsions of nature and society, as James characterized the physical and moral side of man, were replaced by internal ones, aesthetic and creative. Thus the most truly free action was possible only in the last stage of man's development.[19]

Spontaneous action was truly man's, since it successfully combined the external and internal forces.

> In order to prove it an action absolutely mine, you must not only show that it was done by my hand or my external self, but also

---

[15] Henry James, *Moralism and Christianity*, p. 48.

[16] *Ibid.*

[17] Letter to William quoted in Matthiessen, *The James Family*, pp. 118-19.

[18] Perry, *The Thought and Character of William James*, p. 71.

[19] Henry James, *Lectures and Miscellanies*, pp. 102-07.

that this external self did not at the time dominate or overrule my internal self. If these two elements of my personality were not perfectly united, perfectly concurrent, in the action; if the internal self were overruled by the external or *vice versa;* then the action is not truly mine, is not a legitimate progeny of my will and understanding, but a bastard or filius nullius, abhorred of God and man.[20]

James always assumed that the external self, dominated by physical and moral laws, did not conflict with the internal self but was capable of harmonious conjunction with it.

Both natural and moral man failed to express that balance or self-centered action which constituted human personality. The development of an active personality was an extremely difficult task, for life was a deep, dark tragedy.[21] Man had to progress through several very hard stretches of life to achieve the spiritual stage. "The natural inheritance of every one who is capable of spiritual life is an unsubdued forest where the wolf howls and every obscene bird of night chatters."[22]

Henry James, Jr., looking back to his childhood, considered the goal his parents set for him almost impossible to achieve:

Our parents had for us no definite project but to be liberally "good" — in other words so good that the presumption of our being so would literally operate anywhere and anyhow, would really amount in itself to a sort of situated state, a sufficient prime position, and leave other circumstances comparatively irrelevant.[23]

The education of Henry James, Jr., coincided with his father's ideas. A child's world was primarily a physical one, corresponding to the natural world of man. Since God's work was done with the raw materials of human life, with "the very commonest affections and appetites and passions of universal man,"[24] physical necessities were good.

Every appetite and passion of man's nature is good and beautiful, and destined to be fully enjoyed, and a scientific society or fellowship among men would ensure this result, without allowing any compromise of the individual dignity, especially without allowing that fierce and disgusting abandonment of them which

---

[20] Henry James, *Moralism and Christianity,* p. 14.
[21] *Ibid.,* pp. 22-23.
[22] William James, p. 79.
[23] Henry James, Jr., *Notes of a Son and Brother,* p. 66.
[24] Letter to Sarah Blake Sturgis Shaw, quoted in Perry, *The Thought and Character of William James,* p. 33.

disfigures so many of our eminent names in church and state, and which infallibly attests the uncleanness of our present morality.[25]

James was no ascetic; the natural life was a good life and was not to be eliminated. Swedenborg would have agreed with this view. However, it was contrary to certain remnants of Puritan morality which still remained and which merged into the general religious fervor of the mid-nineteenth century, one of the most prudish the world has seen. James's concept of God caused him to follow more liberal lines, for God also could sympathize with feelings of "Love, Friendship, Paternity, and Ambition."[26]

Physical needs were not only good but they were insistent, and many times demanded satisfaction. Thus a starving man felt the need to satisfy his hunger by any means, legitimate or otherwise. Stealing a loaf of bread could not, therefore, be laid to this man's door, since it was physical and not spiritual sin. Perhaps one could call this sin evidence of a depraved nature; most theologies would do so. James denied that the case of stealing was important, since it merely indicated that man's physical nature was out of harmony with his spirit.[27] Physical sin resulted only when man was refused due outlets for his physical needs by his own moral nature or society. The fault did not lie in physical needs, which were intrinsically good; perhaps moral nature or society was to blame.

This was not to suppose that man ought to be overwhelmingly concerned with fleshly satisfactions. James never supposed that man was even predominantly a physical being; he always assumed that man had a higher nature. As a matter of record, "Man, on the other hand, is all selfhood or individuality, so that when we find his physical nature overbearing or coercing his moral quality, we no longer call him man, but idiot."[28] Excessive physical indulgence was the evil, rather than a moderate exercise of the passions.

The physical body might be a great burden at times:

> The material body is needful and good when the soul is materialized or accommodated to it; but in sabbatical moments, when the soul, by some Divine epiphany, finds its keepers asleep and its prison doors unbarred, and goes abroad to drink the immortal airs of Paradise, we feel the material body to be a hin-

[25] Henry James, *Lectures and Miscellanies*, p. 48.
[26] *Ibid.*, p. 400.
[27] Henry James, *Moralism and Christianity*, pp. 17-18.
[28] Henry James, "Faith and Science," p. 367.

drance and a drag, and oftentimes prematurely, no doubt, cry
aloud to be delivered from it. We see very plainly that the best
part of our human experience ever here is unassisted by the
material body, is even impaired by its fellowship; and hence
we might infer very reasonably that spiritual existence in pro-
portion to its perfection, exacts a subtler and more pliant incorporation than consists with material substance.[29]

But even the more unpleasant aspects of physical life functioned in man's development and education. Pain, which was no
stranger to James, aided man in his search for a better, more
spiritual life. James had suffered several leg amputations in his
youth. Since even perfect amputations leave phantom images still
in the mind of the patient, James might be expected to have
experienced this curious sensation. He very neatly incorporated
his impression of his missing leg into his philosophy. James used
his phantom leg to reassure Mrs. Howe that her deceased son
enjoyed some kind of immortality: "I have had a consciousness
of the limb itself all of my life. Although buried and out of sight,
it has always remained a part of me."[30] How convincing this was
to Mrs. Howe is not recorded.

There was no question in James's mind that pain was a good
and not an evil. If man had no experience of pain and only
one of continued, unchanged pleasure, he would remain a vege-
table, characterized by passivity, instead of an animal, characterized by volition.[31] Pain provoked men to action in order to allevi-
ate that pain, and by so doing, forced man not to take nature
for granted.

In addition, nature's refusal to give man satisfaction forced
man to call upon God for help. God had already anticipated that
man would need some help in subjecting the physical world, so
He provided man with the tool to overcome nature, namely,
genius to invent. This provision did not violate the tacit assumptions of creation that God would not appear to give life to the
creature, so the solution was satisfactory to both man and God.[32]
An example of the use of genius was the wooden leg which James
wore in the place of his amputated one; man overcomes nature
by this device. However, suppose a man, rather than being stimulated to creative action by pain, submits to it? Would this not
prove James's diagnosis wrong? James maintained that God

[29] Henry James, *The Nature of Evil*, pp. 304-05.
[30] Julia Ward Howe, *Reminiscences*, p. 325.
[31] Henry James, *The Nature of Evil*, pp. 84-85.
[32] Henry James, *Lectures and Miscellanies*, p. 270.

paid no attention to unmanly defeatism, for man must strive in the world. Nature, however, provided a remedy in extreme cases of physical pain either by temporary loss of consciousness, rendering man insensitive to pain, or by death.[33]

What had man's physical experience proved? In the first place man had been shown that he was not the real power in the universe, because he had to conform to nature in his earlier life.[34] However, later experience showed that man was supreme over nature by reason of his actual control over his physical existence. James took, in the second place, great care to prove that physical pain and life contributed to the educative process.

But if man remained only a physical animal, he was no better than an idiot. If he could not act independently of his natural desires, he was not better than a horse, since the quality distinguishing man from animal was personality, independent action.[35] The instrument that enabled man to change from a physical form to a moral one, to a human personality, was the will. Since the will was a product of the intellect, which was designed to rule the passions and to mould them into acceptable forms,[36] man used his will to temper and control nature.

The moral world consisted of the natural world subjected to the direction of society through the will of the individual. This life was also good, since abstinence from physical excesses was always good.[37] Moral life was the mark of man, just as physical life was the mark of an animal. Whenever man was spoken of, one supposed the moral life.

Since the symbol of moral action was obedience to will or choice,[38] this meant that man had a new responsibility. The moral life involved some conscious self-denial, for man must repress some physical urges to conform better to society. James criticized the old theology, as he called it, for making self-denial the end of life; the moral life, he insisted, had value only as the means to achieve spiritual life, the goal of man.[39] Since morality covered the relationship of an individual to the other members of society, moral action consisted of acknowledging one's obligation to so-

---

[33] *Ibid.*, p. 272.
[34] *Ibid.*, p. 268.
[35] Henry James, *Moralism and Christianity*, p. 12.
[36] Henry James, *Christianity the Logic of Creation*, p. 15.
[37] Henry James, *The Nature of Evil*, pp. 230-31.
[38] Henry James, *Society the Redeemed Form of Man*, p. 13.
[39] Henry James, *Lectures and Miscellanies*, pp. 151-52.

ciety; immoral action resulted when man did not acknowledge this obligation to others.[40]

The difference between physical nature and moral society was not that either lacked coercion; it was merely that the coercive element differed. In the physical stage, natural urges compelled men to certain actions, while in the moral state societal good dominated man's acts. The moral stage ranked higher because man, organized into society, was more important than nature. Neither of these stages was a perfect one, however, since both relied upon external coercion.

Moral life, like physical life, was good inherently; it was evil only in its perversion and excess. Morality educated man; through fear of temporal or spiritual punishment, it taught him not to "commit false or malicious speaking, theft, adultery, murder, or covetousness."[41] Every man had to participate in the moral life, since man learned best through life experiences and only a small portion of truth might be transferred from one mind to another.[42] Man needed the discipline of both the physical and moral life to prepare him for the spiritual one, but those disciplines were to be supplanted by an inner one in the spontaneous stage of man's life.

> The self-hood or moral force, on this theory, becomes trans- formed from an absolute to a contingent existence, from a final to a mediatorial possession of man, and a true cosmology ac- cordingly will no longer start from time and space which are the laws of physical existence merely, but from Infinite Love and Wisdom, which are the source of spiritual existence.[43]

One must be extremely careful not to attribute to James any belief that moral distinctions are not real. He believed that the difference between good and evil was as evident to the rational mind of man as physical differences were to the senses,[44] and that morality was as real and strong as physical passions. Nowhere did James contradict himself on this. Ralph Barton Perry con- ceived of James as a morally indignant man who fought with fervor against the hypocritical elements in his society.[45] This view, in the author's opinion, is essentially correct. Perhaps nothing

---

[40] Henry James, *Moralism and Christianity*, p. 22.
[41] Henry James, *Society the Redeemed Form of Man*, p. 268.
[42] Letter to Emerson, quoted in Perry, *The Thought and Character of William James*, p. 71.
[43] Henry James, *The Nature of Evil*, pp. 293-94.
[44] Henry James, *Christianity the Logic of Creation*, p. 63.
[45] Perry, *The Thought and Character of William James*, p. 162.

illustrates the strong force of morality better than James's own attitude toward the evils that he saw within his own society.

From what has already been said, one might assume that moral evil was not true evil, if moral life was not true life. James propounded this idea, which paralleled his view that physical evil could help man and not hurt him. Moral evil might also educate and help man: "The experience of evil accordingly, which has been inseparable from our rational expansion, is strictly tributary in the Divine wisdom to a good which otherwise would never have dawned upon us.... ."[46]

To discuss the problem of moral evil, James started with man's original creation. Man was then in a state of equilibrium between the forces that would separate him from God and the ones that would unite him with God. Similarly, within society man was at the mercy of competing forces of moral good and evil. James, studying society, noted that these forces varied from one locale to another. The equilibrium had been disturbed in society, so that man might have a preponderance of good or evil influences acting upon him.

While many people interpreted the Declaration of Independence to mean that all men were born equal, James did not:

> The Declaration is guilty of no such absurdity. It does not say that all men are born equal, for it is notorious that they are born under the greatest conceivable inequalities — inequalities of heart and head and hand — inequalities even of physical form and structure.[47]

It quite commonly happened that a man was raised in a section of society in which moral good was de-emphasized and moral evil predominated. Since the individual was coerced by evil influence, his evil actions did not belong to him. True spiritual sin had to be action which grew out of the agreements of man's various natures and was not imposed upon man by either nature or society.

James's view of man was very optimistic, for he never believed that man, in his heart, desired evil. An example of this faith was his description of the punishment that society gave to a man who had broken the law. Particularly, he was concerned with those murderers who were to be executed. What did society's execution imply about the nature of the culprit?

---

[46] Henry James, *Substance and Shadow*, p. 59.

[47] Henry James, "The Social Significance of Our Institutions," *American Philosophic Addresses*, ed. Joseph Blau (New York: Columbia University, 1946), p. 244.

The meaning of it [the execution] is that we do not believe any man to be evil at bottom or in his inmost heart, but only from a lack of outward freedom. . . . If we really believed the man to be bad in himself, bad independently of his physical and social conditions, we should never dare to send him to God.[48]

James assumed that no one would be so cruel to evil as to force it into a direct relation with good. So besides reflecting the essential humanitarianism of James, this passage shows his belief that man was innately good and only perverted by outside forces.

I repeat then that good and evil moral, and pleasure and pain physical, are facts which fall within the strictly constitutional plane of human life, and hence do not supply the conception of spiritual evil, or that which separates the soul from God. For example, there is no man living who is not constitutionally liable to falsehood, to theft, to adultery, to murder, and to covetousness. . . . So on the other hand there is no person of average physical and mental health, who is not constitutionally liable to gentleness, kindness, patience, generosity, magnanimity, on the presentation of adequate motives. . . . Hence we are not inwardly or spiritually chargeable with this good and evil; they are common to the race of men, and we are consequently forbidden to make any appropriation of them.[49]

Man's inability to claim moral good or evil as his own was of tremendous importance to James because he had found a logical inconsistency in the idea of personal morality. The inconsistency was this: if a man worked diligently to fulfill divine ordinance and to improve his moral standards, this same man could not avoid violating the law that he was trying to keep. Since James assumed that the impulse to perfect oneself implied a goal of lifting oneself above the average of mankind, a man striving to be good was covetous, desiring something for himself which other men could not have. So in the end the moral law was broken, and the striving individual was full of the "profoundest spiritual humiliation and despair."[50] Fulfilling the moral law was impossible; man had no hope of that.

There was, however, great danger in the moral realm, a danger much greater than anything encountered in the physical realm. Since the moral element was inextricably connected with selfhood or the belief in every man that his actions were his own,[51] self-

[48] Henry James, *Moralism and Christianity,* pp. 18-19.
[49] Henry James, *The Nature of Evil,* pp. 75-76.
[50] Henry James, *The Secret of Swedenborg,* p. 163.
[51] Henry James, *Substance and Shadow,* p. 3.

hood might be overemphasized. Morality always implied that man was absolute in himself;[52] if this became a permanent article of faith, man could commit the one sin of which he was capable, the assumption that he was separate from God. Thus the moral stage of man's life had this great danger hanging over it, the danger that man would become spiritually sinful.

Most moralists who tried to improve their behavior assumed unconsciously that one man has the capacity to become better spiritually than another man. Theologians who shared this view made a much more dangerous mistake, since they attributed the difference to the regeneration of man, thus enlisting God on the side of spiritual inequality.[53] Moralists merely assumed that moral capacity was a product of nature, a less pernicious error. The moralists' assumption was wrong; but the theological position was heretical, since James always insisted that God paid no attention to personal distinction.

James hated no one as much as a self-righteous person; he loved to puncture such a person's sanctimonious pretense. "The gentleman is the apotheosis or glorified form of the devil," James insisted.[54] Again, James indicated that a familiar group of people existed whose attitude was so stultifyingly pious as to create the sense of inferiority in everyone else: "One continually meets persons of this sort from whose company he retires no less bruised and defrauded spiritually, than others do physically from the company of some renowned boxer."[55]

The sign of these excessively moral individuals was a self-defeating piety. Their piety was not an honest kind, the pursuit of one's everyday vocation; but rather it was a direct, aggressive piety. The outpouring of an unreconciled heart, this piety "drives a man to the perpetual gymnastic of praise, prayer, and self-sacrifice, in order to win favor not yet bestowed: is awfully deleterious. . . ."[56] Morally proud people possessed tenuous intellects and hearts of "impenetrable hardness," and they lived lives "of complete selfishness."[57] James compared these individuals to the mildew on flowers and complained that he came away from such people feeling that half of his vital power had been taken.[58]

---

[52] William James, pp. 43-45.
[53] Henry James, *Society the Redeemed Form of Man*, p. 414.
[54] Henry James, *Substance and Shadow*, p. 254.
[55] Henry James, *The Church of Christ Not an Ecclesiasticism*, p. 46.
[56] Henry James, *The Nature of Evil*, pp. 124-25.
[57] Henry James, *Lectures and Miscellanies*, pp. 212-13.
[58] *Ibid.*

James always insisted that moral life was good if not carried to extremes, for it was through the medium of selfhood that redemption was at last accomplished.[59] He followed Swedenborg in holding that there was a great distinction between a natural and a perverted love of self, just as there was between a natural and a perverted love for the world.[60] Both physical and moral life would be incorporated into spiritual life, but precautions must be taken so that these sections do not take all the space, leaving no room for the spiritual life.

The presence of moral evil may contribute to the development of a spiritual life, which comes from the moral life aided by conscience. James defined the conscience in the following way: "Conscience, or the knowledge of good and evil, is a phenomenon which marks the infancy of human culture. It has its origin in the limitation which the senses impose upon the infantile consciousness of man."[61]

Conscience was a badge of man's fallen nature; man received it when he presumed to self-sufficiency:

> Accordingly, God endows him man with conscience, or the sentiment of responsibility (in scriptural phrase, *sends him forth from Eden*), and devolves upon this flaming viceregent the task of humbling his conceit, and bringing him at last into the obedience of truth.[62]

Even though conscience was the keynote of moral life, it contained within itself the seeds of its own destruction. One of the reasons for this suicidal nature was that conscience, originally designated as a synonym for selfhood, also had a social nature. Obedience to the moral law had lifted man from the physical realm into the moral realm, ending the period of man's inhumanity to man as dictated by nature.[63] After its original function, conscience betrayed itself and was symbolic of social control.

> Man, on the other hand, is under law exclusively to what he calls conscience, which is a sentiment he feels in his own bosom of his profound individuality or difference from all other men, and at the same time of his profound identity or community with them. Conscience is always the explicit attestation of a harmony of interests between man and man. It is thus an essen-

---

[59] Henry James, *Society the Redeemed Form of Man*, p. 449.
[60] *Ibid.*, p. 191.
[61] Henry James, *Lectures and Miscellanies*, p. 168.
[62] Henry James, *The Church of Christ Not an Ecclesiasticism*, p. 67.
[63] William James, p. 218.

tially social force; being, indeed, the invincible Divine pledge and germ of a frank and lustrous society, fellowship or equality. . . .[64]

Conscience, therefore, told man that he was not independent, but rather dependent upon the cooperation of his neighbors.

Conscience helped to translate the moral world into the spiritual world in additional ways. Since its function was always negative, always designed to give men a sense of sin and never to reassure men of their spiritual health,[65] the most active conscience ought to belong to those who were most morally reprehensible. Thus the morally proud man should possess the most tender and active conscience. But by empirical test James concluded that this was not the case. The exact opposite seemed more nearly true, for those who have done the least wrong have the most tender consciences; and although they may be almost innocent, they nevertheless retained a deep feeling of sinfulness. How could this be explained? James, after considering the problem, decided that "the sense of sin is at bottom only a tough earthly rudiment and root of spiritual reverence of humility. . . ."[66]

Conscience enabled man to have a sense of inability, for by its light man saw how pitifully inadequate it was as a device for union with God. If man attempted to become perfect morally, he committed the sin of covetousness; and the more perfect he became, the more sinful he confessed himself to be. Man had no hope of achieving true manhood in the realm of the moral world.

The man with the tender conscience was well on his way to spiritual life. A true confession of sin, one marked by privacy, was the first step toward leaving the moral level for the spiritual.[67] Confessing sin in public was not practicable, since men never meant what they publicly confessed. A private confession of sin was not easy, but it was necessary.

Christ Himself befriended those who confessed themselves to be sinners and was an inveterate enemy of morally self-righteous people.[68] The reason was simple: those who proclaimed themselves to be sinners were using their consciences as they were supposed to be used. Man had a conscience that functioned to remind him of his separation from God; man was not supposed to use his

[64] Henry James, Review of Bushnell's *Vicarious Sacrifice, North American Review,* CII (1866), 567.

[65] Henry James, *The Secret of Swedenborg,* pp. 150-53.

[66] Henry James, *Substance and Shadow,* p. 179.

[67] *Ibid.,* pp. 182-83.

[68] Henry James, *The Nature of Evil,* p. 146.

conscience as an agent which gained "peace and reconciliation."[69]

> And HE Christ taught His disciples the same contempt for the law as a justifying economy. The only knowledge Jesus Christ ever claimed as at all peculiar to Him (and this is altogether peculiar, leaving Him not only without a rival among men, but without a second) was that God's law given to any people could only be a ministry of death to its subjects, inasmuch as it was not literal but spiritual, and therefore took no note of the utmost personal differences among them, but commanded all men without exception who could spiritually win its approval to *qualify themselves* as He did, *by dying to it,* and to every literal and fallacious lust engendered by it.[70]

The example of Christ indicated the way to spiritual manhood, since spiritual man would lose the consciousness of sin which was the bane of moral existence.[71] As the new man was an inward one, action would no longer be judged within a moral framework. Man's "only proper expression or clothing therefore is freedom, not force; is spontaneity, not will; is goodness, not truth."[72]

The most particularly different aspect of a spiritual life was the perfect equality of this life. The new man contained all the elements of the race; he was the composite of all individuals.[73] While physical man was separated from the rest of his fellows by physical strength, beauty, and ability, and while moral man was separated from the rest of the world by his actions, good or bad, the spiritual man would be united with his brother, as both were equally dependent upon God or upon the instinct within themselves. The visible characteristics of spiritual man were his equality and consequent unity with the rest of society.[74]

The unity of mankind culminates James's thought, for man learns to become a man only as he becomes more social. An animal remains an animal because of his physical constitution, while only men are capable of becoming cultural beings.[75] Spiritual man was never to be considered out of relation to his fellow man or be singled out for special praise or blame. On the other hand, the race had no existence apart from the individuals who composed it, for if the race had separate existence, as the individuals who constituted it had, it would also have good and

[69] *Ibid.*
[70] William James, p. 235.
[71] *Ibid.,* p. 184.
[72] *Ibid.,* p. 236.
[73] *Ibid.,* p. 362.
[74] James, quoted in Grattan, *The Three Jameses,* p. 59.
[75] Henry James, Review of Bushnell's *Vicarious Sacrifice,* p. 567.

evil properties.[76] James denied that this was possible; the race was neutral in itself. Man was still the measure of all things, but only within the context of his unity with other men.

What were to be the characteristics of spiritual man? First, the individual who entered the spiritual life will have had a true piety — "a piety attuned to the ministries of science, organized observation of nature and society,"[77] and "a piety which celebrates God no longer as the mere traditional source of lapsed and contingent felicities, but as the present and palpable doer of divinest deeds — such as feeding the starving earth's population, etc. . . ."[78] The new piety, in other words, will be active and outgoing. It will not seek personal identification with God but rather unity with the rest of mankind.

True righteousness, rising out of true piety, was not the "filthy righteousness" that came from physical or moral law, but rather the spontaneous righteousness that came from the Divine-Natural-Humanity, which contained elements of physical and moral law.[79] The new righteousness, like the new piety, was quite simple; it consisted of participation by the individual in the "spirit of humanity or universal love,"[80] and the temper of spiritual man was a humanitarian one. James even suggested that the sole test Jesus used to determine those who had true faith in His teachings was their attitude toward their fellow man.[81] The Calvinists would not have agreed with James, but perhaps the Transcendentalists would.

Since self-love in the spiritual man was diminished so that little of the aggressive element remained to contest neighborly love, spiritual man had the major virtue of humility, as contrasted with the pride of physical and moral man.[82] The new man would be so humble that he could be identified by the fact that he was the least discriminating about the differences between men, as far as intrinsic worth was concerned.[83]

While disbelief in personal worth was a mark of spiritual man, this same individual had a high opinion of man taken as a whole.

[76] Henry James, *The Secret of Swedenborg*, p. 59.

[77] Henry James, *Lectures and Miscellanies*, p. 144.

[78] James, quoted in Stephen Pearl Andrews and Horace Greeley, *Love, Marriage, and Divorce and the Sovereignty of the Individual* (New York: Stringer and Townsend, 1853), p. 29.

[79] Henry James, *Lectures and Miscellanies*, pp. 237-38.

[80] *Ibid.*, p. 381.

[81] *Ibid.*, pp. 205-06.

[82] Henry James, *Substance and Shadow*, p. 192.

[83] Henry James, *The Church of Christ Not an Ecclesiasticism*, p. 49.

Man himself is the supreme fact, and not any mere quality or accident pertaining to him. ... Man is essentially above praise, because being God-made, being God-informed, to use a scholastic expression, he is really above all appreciation. ... To be man therefore is to be virtuous and beautiful. Virtue is only a classical name for manhood. The two words mean the same thing, and no virtue exists which humanity does not imply.[84]

When he spoke of humility, James did not mean that man did not have qualities of which he ought to be proud. He merely wanted to include all men in this pride.

Looking back into the historic past, James observed that society elevated certain classes almost to sacred positions. These classes were the following: (1) priests, who had a religious and educative function; (2) soldiers, who had a military duty to protect a country from foreign aggression; and (3), most recently, merchants and commercial men, who ran the nation's business.[85] In particular, the priest and the king (who was the chief of the warriors) had been accorded the greatest reverence and honor. Man, with his increasing intelligence and social knowledge, will, James thought, eventually come to partake of the function of priest and king.[86] Puritan thinkers, too, had assured their followers that they combined secular and sacerdotal powers; James, however, extended these powers to every man.

In spite of his emphasis upon society as the redeemed form of man, James never relinquished his idea that man's own identity ought never to be violated. Man should always retain his individuality and will in fact do so. In commenting upon Stirling's defense of Hegel against charges of pantheism, in which Stirling maintained that Hegel was not a materialist, even if he held views close to pantheism, James concluded: "As if the most abject materialism, as if to wallow with the pigs, and still preserve one's identity were not infinitely preferable to being absorbed by another personality, even were that personality God."[87] In the perfect society each man will be separate, even though the fact of human unity will be uppermost in his mind. For life was individuality of character, which cannot be given to one since it was a product of long educational development.[88]

---

[84] Henry James, *Lectures and Miscellanies,* pp. 72-74.
[85] Henry James, "Woman and the Woman's Movement," pp. 283-84.
[86] Henry James, *Lectures and Miscellanies,* pp. 18-19.
[87] Henry James, Review of Stirling's *Secret of Hegel,* p. 267.
[88] James's letter to Mrs. Francis G. Shaw, quoted in Perry, *The Thought and Character of William James,* p. 158.

Since the trait that distinguished man was not action under constraint of physical or moral considerations but rather spiritual action, action dictated by man's own ideal of good, truth and beauty,[89] the man most prominent in the association of spiritual men would be the genius:

> In short, let genius become the hierarchical principle, and constitute the sole measure of one's social distinction; and society would instantly become orderly. For genius (by which term all along you observe I mean nothing technical in man, but simply his power of ideal action, his faculty of acting without reference either to passions or appetites, and solely with reference to the infinite beauty, the infinite goodness and truth, which animates his soul) constitutes the real presence of God in man, and all men therefore acknowledge it with spontaneous devotion.[90]

Man's genius was not something to be proud of, since it was a product of many accidental factors. Those who possess genius are ashamed of it insofar as they are imbued with spiritual considerations,[91] for they realize that an ideal association requires that all men be equally important regardless of their contributions to that association. Genius might be dangerous if it led to a sense of superiority and inferiority.

Freedom was the most important attribute of man's spiritual nature, according to James. "Freedom is his birthright as man, not as Roman or Lutheran, not as Greek or Arabian, not as English or American."[92] Spiritual man's essential virtue was freedom. Freedom distinguished man from animal, for although the passions restricting the physical action of man and the appetites of animals were roughly equivalent, the passions were man's lowest stage and animal's highest stage.[93] Only man could rise above these appetites to free action. One is even led to conclude that a man behaving spontaneously was a spiritual man.

James attempted to prove that the only true life was the spontaneous one. Life, according to James, was not contradictory; man did not act in such a way as to permanently harm himself. Therefore, "Human life, in a word, is not primarily natural; does not acknowledge a physical origin: or we should have no suicide. Neither is it primarily moral, flowing from a social origin: or we

---

[89] Henry James, *Lectures and Miscellanies*, p. 346.
[90] *Ibid.*
[91] Henry James, *Moralism and Christianity*, p. 55.
[92] Henry James, *The Church of Christ Not an Ecclesiasticism*, pp. 92-93.
[93] Henry James, "Faith and Science," p. 367.

should be destitute of moral evil."[94] Reflection upon this assumption gives one the impression that once again James has displayed an extremely high opinion of human nature, one with which Freudians would probably now disagree. Harmony within the universe began with the nature of man, which does not war against itself.

What factors composed spontaneous action and how did they operate? Again James called upon science to inaugurate the good life and proceeded to define that life as combining instinct and will, with neither superior over the other.[95] Not only was man's spontaneous life harmonic within itself, but it also combined harmoniously elements of will and instinct. This assumption paralleled James's belief that a man acting spontaneously would also act in a physically and morally acceptable way.

The antithesis of spontaneity was habit. If spontaneity was intrinsically good, habit was intrinsically bad. Since habit was, at best, a surrogate for original action, it was bad to the degree that the same original action was good. But since James had already argued for a universe in which all attributes are equally important, although not identical, it must follow that the most innocent habits had the same spiritual affect as the most vicious ones. James illustrated this principle by the example of the very acceptable, popular habit of regular church attendance and participation in prayer, which James maintained did as much spiritual damage as "others of whatever conventional odium."[96] Thus, one would be forced to conclude that going to church was as bad as taking opium, provided, of course, that both were done by force of habit.

The sphere in which man acted with perfect spontaneity was the sphere of art.[97]

> Art, then, or the use accomplished by man as of himself and not of natural or accidental constraint, is, according to the new theology, the divine end in humanity; and the evolution of this end is exclusively social. Art is thus the distinctive glory of man. It is what defines the Creator's abode within him, and gives him the lordship of the lower creation.[98]

Art served as a constant reminder to man that he was unified in

---

[94] Henry James, *Christianity the Logic of Creation*, p. 103.
[95] *Ibid.*, p. 15.
[96] Henry James, *Lectures and Miscellanies*, pp. 427-28.
[96] *Ibid.*, p. 102.
[97] *Ibid.*
[98] Henry James, "Swedenborg as a Theologian," pp. 302-03.

the race; this was its excuse for existence. All that defined a work of art was whether it was complete within itself, whether the object and the subject agreed.[99] Art was the action of man that perfectly fitted his spontaneous nature, and hence a simple shoe repair job might qualify as a work of art.

"Thus our true individuality is neither physical nor moral. It is purely aesthetic. It stands in our relation neither to nature nor to our fellow-man, but exclusively to God, who is our inmost life."[100] Every man had an obligation to become an artist, that is, to work from an inner ideal which helped to illustrate some social beauty or use.[101] The artist acted by virtue of his internal, aesthetic compulsions along lines which promoted his physical or moral welfare; yet, physical and moral welfare were not the prime considerations. If man behaved in such a way as to indicate that his motives were primarily physical or moral, under the compulsion of appetite or duty, he was, according to James, an artisan, not an artist.[102] This rule had universal application, from laborers to poets; if either of these worked because he was so compelled, he was no artist.

Perhaps the best example of the artist and his art, or of man and his spontaneous action, was given by James when he discussed the waiter who often served him. This man did nothing out of the ordinary; it was his attitude alone that distinguished him:

> No, it is exclusively the way in which it [the meal] is set before me, a way altogether peculiar to this man, which attests that in doing it he is not thinking either of earning his wages, or doing his duty towards me, but only of satisfying his own conception of beauty with the resources before him.[103]

In the new society all men would act from such a motive. As they acted from the inner compulsion of beauty, duty would also be fulfilled, because when every man served taste and beauty, duty took care of itself.[104] The perfect fellowship that was inevitably coming would satisfy both the requirements of public interest, duty, and the requirements of private interest, beauty. One ought to keep this point in mind, for it was a very necessary part of James's thought.

[99] Henry James, *Lectures and Miscellanies,* pp. 111-12.

[100] Henry James, "Socialism and Civilization," p. 57.

[101] Henry James, *Lectures and Miscellanies,* p. 113.

[102] Henry James, *Moralism and Christianity,* p. 25.

[103] Henry James, "A Scientific Statement of the Lord of Divine Man," *Massachusetts Quarterly Review,* p. 3.

[104] Henry James, *Lectures and Miscellanies,* p. 362.

James had never supposed that all men acting without any compulsion, save natural ones, would have the same tastes, since the moral and physical education that men had varied from one area to another: "Of course then we must expect infinite varieties of genius or power ranging from that of the highest seraph to that of the humblest clod. But all will be linked together in a perfectly human unity."[105] Essential confusion existed, James decided, over the two concepts of unity and universality. The two ideas were not synonymous, as most people had supposed. Unity was what all men had in common. The analogy James used to illustrate unity was a physiological one: all parts contribute to the whole to form a perfect unity[106] as all parts of the body contribute to a human being. This does not mean that the parts were universal ones which could be interchanged, for an eye cannot serve as a leg. Men are equal in importance, but they are not the same.

James assumed that the ideal individual would be completely independent: "no human being can afford to commit his happiness to another's keeping."[107] It was a necessary condition for the perfect society that man should be free to do as he pleased. Not even love should make man too dependent; James often lamented the restrictive nature of his love for his children, for this hindered his freedom to give himself to them freely. James was convinced that no man could be dependent upon another for any period of time without becoming "degraded out of his just human proportions."[108] If this was true, the greatest help one man could give another would be to leave that man alone. Since man learned only by his own experiences, he might find less use for libraries,[109] but this would be good.

The only premise on which so extreme a statement of individual liberty can rest is that one man's creative action could not injure another. James believed this for two reasons. First, he believed that as man acted spontaneously he had no desire to take the good name, the physical or moral status, and the property of another.[110] Second, he believed that spontaneous action would demonstrate no conflict between the interest of one man and that of another.

---

[105] *Ibid.,* p. 82.

[106] Henry James, "The Philosophy of the Heart," Letter to Francis Ellingwood Abbot, *The Index,* VII (1876), 231.

[107] Henry James, Letter to Mrs. Tappan quoted in Perry, *The Thought and Character of William James,* p. 58.

[108] *Ibid.,* p. 237.

[109] *Ibid.,* p. 58.

[110] Henry James, *Lectures and Miscellanies,* pp. 34-35.

James indicated that he could never "be really harmed by any other person's entire freedom to do as he pleases, or really profited by his partial restraint."[111] The universe was a harmonious place, where no actions on the spontaneous level ever clashed.

Perhaps no more startling or extreme statements of the nature of man have ever been more consistently made and elaborated than those of James. Man's physical appetites and moral sanctions were intrinsically good, and bad only when he indulged in these actions too vigorously. Man, acting spontaneously, could do no wrong; he could harm no one, himself or others. He was and should be free to do anything he pleased, for this would be the right thing. One could scarcely conceive of a more radical belief in the innate goodness of man. The Transcendentalists and Unitarians had supposed man to be good as he consciously chose moral good, while James freed man from the necessity of choice.[112] Man need not choose anything since his involuntary actions are good.

James's postulation of man's freedom has been taken by most of his critics to indicate a rather pronounced antinomianism. One should, however, make several reservations. The first is that man must act spontaneously in order to be free; Christ made this possible by His Sacrifice, symbolically interpreted. However, spontaneous action presumably could be forthcoming from those who had no knowledge of either Christ or Christianity. As a matter of fact, since the whole race was to be saved, some that would be gathered up would not have had this revelation.

The religious, redemptive movement which James described was accomplished on the secular level and could be equated with the growth of knowledge. As man grew more aware of his past and of the world that surrounded him, the greater was the possibility of his becoming aware of the spontaneous life, since it was his action alone which determined, in the end, whether he was spiritually saved or not. Spontaneous action also foretold of the future when everyone possessed such an attribute. All progress in this direction was made with the knowledge of God, for He had given man the necessary equipment to judge and understand the world.

Moreover, within the new society where man was free to act as he pleased, some men might still live in spiritual sin. Men might act spontaneously but assume that *they* were responsible

---

[111] Henry James, "Is Marriage Holy?" *Atlantic Monthly*, XXV (1869), p. 365.

[112] Henry James, *Society the Redeemed Form of Man*, p. 13.

for the good they did, and thus qualify themselves for hell in the old system. However, if these men recognized the social nature of their universe and continued to act in an artistic, aesthetic fashion, they would be free to act any way they might feel.

Few traditional Christian thinkers would have assumed so much. Certainly the idea that all men, acting on impulse, would have behaved in a spiritual manner would have been foreign to them. A medieval Christian would have held that all necessary functions of society are of equal value, but he could hardly have concluded from this that man would not injure his own nature or that of others if freed from physical and moral coercion.

The primary ideas in James's social philosophy came from his religious conviction that men were free and good, and these ideas, finally, governed his view of social institutions. James often assumed that the value of an institution was in direct ratio to its ability to further the ideal of freedom. It is in this particular sense that James's continued emphasis upon the goodness of freed human nature becomes important.

Five

Society and Institutions

Someday man will be spontaneously creative, James concluded. Thus, in the final analysis man will not be restricted by either the physical limits of nature or the moral limits of society; he will be limited only by the range of his own impulses. So the results of the history of both nature and society were foreordained for James, as man was destined to become superior to nature and society.[1] This was not the sole result of the operation of time, nor was it the most important. More important than man's dominance over nature was man's worthiness, through inward power, of this dominance, as he achieved knowledge for salvation and redemption.[2]

When James reviewed the universe, he concluded that within this universe everything was significant. Nothing existed by accident.[3] It was with the premises of the perfectibility of man and the significance of all of life that James interpreted the major factors of human life, nature and society.

Experience within man's own environment proved not only necessary, but good. Reason, as James indicated, illuminated every event to give it meaning, but reason needed experience upon which to operate.[4] Since prime importance lay in race experience, the history of man was invaluable. When James defined history, he spoke in almost Hegelian language:

> What we call history is only an instinctive effort of the common or associated mind of the race, to put on form, to come to self-consciousness, to realize its own majestic unity, by means of

---

[1] Henry James, *Moralism and Christianity,* p. 45.
[2] Henry James, *Lectures and Miscellanies,* p. 282.
[3] Henry James, *The Secret of Swedenborg,* p. 13.
[4] Henry James, *Christianity the Logic of Creation,* p. 24.

the purchase afforded it in the experience of the individual bosom.[5]

Man learned freely from his life on earth; for if man had to have life and experience forced upon him, the presumption would be that he was independent of God and could resist divine influx.[6] Human history, then, must contain nothing "arbitrary or fortuitous." From this followed the idea that history could in no conceivable way have been different than it was,[7] for history was nothing less than the revelation of God in time.[8] Human history spelled out man's rise to the Divine-Natural-Humanity and deserved study as one of the most important factors in man's education for divinity. James's teleological view of history differed little from traditional Christian views that showed God operating in the world, except that it almost completely disguised God in the operations of man. James, after reading Henry C. Carey's book on political economy, concluded that both he and Carey agreed that there was a constant law operating in the universe. This law graded down the higher classes of society and graded up the lower, so that the extremes of society became more equal.[9] This was according to divine intention.

History was metaphysical in origin. Another branch of knowledge dealt with empirical information; this was science.[10] Science and history displayed different, discrete qualities, with history using scientific fact to support James's conclusion that society was progressing toward equality. James displayed a respect for science which would have done credit to a completely naturalistic mind, but he always insisted that science, attractive as it was, keep within its own rather rigidly defined area.

Science also appeared inferior to the religious intelligence that operated in history, since science relied upon the observation of outward phenomena while religion utilized inward consciousness to verify and interpret scientific facts.[11] Scientific intelligence depended upon external stimuli to work and was, therefore, unfree. If James's premise that freedom was the highest quality is accepted, one must admit that science had little claim to being the queen of the intellectual world.

---

[5] Henry James, *Substance and Shadow,* p. 461.
[6] Henry James, *The Nature of Evil,* p. 63.
[7] Henry James, *Lectures and Miscellanies,* p. 58.
[8] Henry James, *Society the Redeemed Form of Man,* pp. 173-74.
[9] Henry James, *The Church of Christ Not an Ecclesiasticism,* pp. 154-55.
[10] Henry James, *Society the Redeemed Form of Man,* p. 111.
[11] William James, ed., *The Literary Remains of Henry James,* p. 280.

Science, the "organized observation of nature and society,"[12] which included social as well as physical science, might lead to several critical intellectual errors. One of the most dangerous of these errors was caused by the scientist's preoccupation with the world of fact. As a result of their concentration on the outside world, scientists often assumed and taught that this world possessed a reality of its own, that it was self-explanatory.[13]

The task of science did not include the right to build a philosophical basis which pretended to explain the world. Other, more qualified men were working at this task. Science dealt with empirical facts, or the appearance of truth to the senses,[14] and that was all. Only two very specific subdivisions of the general task of science were proper grounds for investigation. These two categories included facts and the relation of facts to each other as organized by the mind,[15] a good example being cause and effect.

Every evolving science was optimistic and predicated a rosy future. The scientific mind, in the end, will be emancipated from the restrictions that were imposed upon it, restrictions such as natural prejudice, authority, routine, and custom.[16] As the perfect society emerges, science will no longer be captive to ephemeral, man-made restrictions and will be incorporated into the new society; science will become philosophy. Even institutional modes of thought will change to allow man more freedom in an ideal society.

Science had a specific job, however, in James's own world. James saw that science was goal-oriented and that the goal had two facets, one negative and the other positive. The negative goal attributed a reality to the phenomenal world which it did not actually possess, which, however, man needed in order to gain selfhood.[17]

The positive function of science dictated a conclusion, a conclusion drawn from a study of the relationship of facts to each other; this conclusion James thought inevitable. The relationship of facts demonstrated harmony in the universe. "The harmonies of creation are the theme of science, and if these harmonies, according to the New Theology, only reflect those which are un-

---

12 Henry James, *Lectures and Miscellanies*, p. 144.
13 William James, p. 330.
14 Henry James, *Society the Redeemed Form of Man*, p. 31.
15 *Ibid.*, p. 225.
16 Henry James, *Christianity the Logic of Creation*, pp. 52-53.
17 Henry James, Review of Alfred Russel Wallace's *Contributions to the Theory of Natural Selection, Atlantic Monthly*, XXVI (1870), 758.

created or absolute, it follows of course that science has no other task than the illustration of Deity."[18] James placed a conclusion upon the speculations of science; and if scientific fact revealed no such conclusion, James insisted that these facts had not been properly considered.

Universal science, the science of correspondents,[19] occupied the highest niche in the hierarchy of scientific knowledge. James defined universal science as the interpretation of scientific facts in a revelatory manner, so as to arrive at a concept of God. This, in the author's opinion, equals religion, as James defined it, and reveals his attempt to reconcile science and religion. As a result of a superior-inferior relationship, no conflict existed between the two, for religion was concerned with the inner life and science with outward experience.[20]

Attempting to make religion a science would have earned James the reputation of negating the scientific method, if he had persistently maintained this attitude in a scientific society. However, if he had lived in a theocratic one, his assumptions would be quite acceptable. Rather than a revolutionary concept of history or science, James had almost a reactionary one. Although he bridged two eras, the romantic and naturalistic, he remained essentially a romantic, sharing some concepts with the Transcendental mind while maintaining other connections with the new naturalism.

A case in point was James's interpretation of the then new theory of evolution, as inspired by Charles Darwin's reflections upon natural selection. James took the theory of evolution as it was applied to the natural world and modified the idea with the supposition that his changes led to a more accurate concept than did the original, unrefined theory. Specifically, James evaluated evolution and concluded that it confirmed his original hypothesis on creation, that there was no single absolute creation but rather a continuous evolutionary one.[21] James welcomed evolutionary theory as proof for his own systematic cosmology.

The evolutionary exponents, Huxley and Haeckle, however, had made one false supposition which greatly perverted their thinking. These men had supposed that evolution had objective reality. This was wrong, for evolution was a subjective product of man's striving to find meaning in the world.[22] The concept of

---

[18] Henry James, *Lectures and Miscellanies,* p. 153.
[19] Henry James, *Moralism and Christianity,* p. 7.
[20] Henry James, "Spiritualism New and Old," p. 359.
[21] Henry James, Review of Wallace's *Contributions,* p. 757.
[22] William James, p. 282.

evolution like the concept of nature was an abstraction that man formulated, and had no existence outside of his mind. Evolutionists had missed the only real meaning of evolution, its influence on the mind of man in search of truth. Nowhere did James presume to criticize evolutionary thought on scientific grounds, for he considered himself incapable of such specialized analysis.

Agreeing that man had evolved from lower animal forms, James took as the primary evolutionary factor not the theory of natural selection but the innate divine element in man that was asserting itself. The divine element was present only in man; it could not be found in animals. James then argued that man was different in kind from animals and that man's evolution from a certain physical form did not imply identity with that form.[23] Man and animal may have been closer to each other at an earlier epoch, but never had they been identical. The maintenance of man's unique position in the created universe seemed a necessary axiom for James.

Evolution, considered in this light, merely proved what James had said all along, that science, as well as history, showed the progression of man toward his perfect goal. Evolution in the physical realm suggested a philosophical counterpart that bolstered James's claim that science had confirmed his theories: "For to men of science generally the doctrine of evolution imports merely the development of one natural species or kind; whereas a true or philosophical doctrine of evolution implies the conversion of natural (or lower) substance into spiritual (or higher) form."[24] Growth was to occur principally in the mind.

Given James's ideas of what history and science proved, let us now turn to nature and society, which science and history interpreted. These states in which man lived, it must be remembered, were both necessary, so that, just as in man, institutional forms progressed through stages which were good in themselves but which gave way to higher states.

Nature also had an important function for man, as it was part of physical existence, all of which had meaning. What did man learn from nature? The physical world functioned merely to provide a meeting ground between man and God,[25] and resulted when man tried to give form to the world in which he lived.

Nature functioned by giving objectivity to all physically existing things through man's imagination. In short, nature was a fiction

---

[23] Henry James, *Society the Redeemed Form of Man,* pp. 288-89.
[24] *Ibid.,* p. 220.
[25] William James, p. 28.

invented by man, an abstraction he used for purposes of clarity. Nature, for James, merely stood for the idea man used when he tried to relate all physical objects together. He realized that nature as such had no existence save in man's classifying mind.[26] Nature was a concept man imposed upon the world to give it meaning.

Abstractions such as nature would not have been necessary if man had actually believed in spiritual creation. "For then," says James, "we should see all the various forms of sense acknowledging a unitary human substance, and would regard any brute unintelligible quantity like what we call Nature, a sheer superfluity or superstition."[27] However, since man was not immediately capable of such belief, the concept of nature remained a necessary tool for men. As far as the divine mind was concerned, the natural universe did not exist;[28] only man made the mistake of giving the universe actual existence.

The physical universe functioned for the mind by giving man form and appearance in contrast to God who gave being.[29] Also it gave man the feeling of being discrete from his fellows. Nature served as mediator between God and man — not, however, in the same sense as the Transcendentalists understood the term. Nature reflected, in the realm of time and space, the constant adjustment between man and God,[30] God giving His bounty and man existing in his necessity. James professed to be able to distinguish between the African and the Englishman by the characteristics they displayed in their natural surroundings. James was not an environmental determinist but the reverse, believing the condition of man was reflected in nature.

Besides functioning as a symbol, nature also functioned as an educative experience.

> If accordingly nature did not exist or appear to me in all her sensibly contrasted forms of light and dark, hot and cold, high and low, hard and soft, rough and smooth, great and small, strong and innocent and noxious, pleasant and painful, my animal sensibilities would afford no anchorage to moral instincts of good and evil in human character, upon which all my subsequent knowledge of spiritual, celestial, and divine things are of necessity to be moulded.[31]

---

[26] Henry James, "Faith and Science," p. 349.
[27] Matthiessen, *The James Family*, pp. 117-18.
[28] Henry James, *The Secret of Swedenborg*, p. 187.
[29] Henry James, *The Church of Christ Not an Ecclesiasticism*, pp. 57-58.
[30] Henry James, *The Secret of Swedenborg*, p. 15.
[31] *Ibid.*

Life taught man how to differentiate in many ways, this differentiation being an essential basis for institutional life. Nature also taught men other important truths. Man, after searching through the realm of nature, becomes aware that everything within this area is mortal, including himself. This convinced men, according to James, that there must be an infallible immortal who contrasted with mortal nature.[32] In an inverse way nature returned man to God by forcing man to doubt his own independent status and by impressing him with his own feeble mortality.

When James viewed the animals that populated the earth, he came to another rather unique conclusion. He denied that animals had any spiritual life. Therefore, he said, their purpose must be to educate man. It followed that these animals represented different kinds of human thought and affection.[33] Some men thought and acted like lions; others could be compared with the dove or the kid. Animals functioned only to exhibit some of man's qualities to him.

Perfected nature would be "the very image of reason, the very mode of order."[34] These qualities would symbolize the degree of perfection which man had achieved. When men became perfectly ordered and rational, nature would mirror this perfection. Difficult and hostile natural surroundings indicated that the men who lived there were in a low stage of spirituality. The ordered landscapes of England proved that' the English were more spiritually advanced than the Africans, who lived among tangled jungles.

Nature also hinted at social relationships. While nature's main function was to provide man with a feeling of particularity, it also gave man a sense of community and set him on the direct road to human fellowship. Man soon discovered that nature required every man to eat, drink, and protect himself,[35] and also provided that each man should die. This natural, unifying sense of common needs and destiny created a base from which man could develop his true individuality.[36]

Since the physical universe reflected man and since man was in a state of flux, nature, too, must be evolving rather than static. Because nature changed to reflect man, science could never com-

---

[32] William James, p. 253.

[33] Henry James, *The Secret of Swedenborg*, p. 35.

[34] Henry James, *Lectures and Miscellanies*, p. 155.

[35] Henry James, "The Radical Dogmatics," *The Radical*, II (1867), 85.

[36] Mrs. John T. Sargent, *Sketches and Reminiscences of the Radical Club* (Boston: James R. Osgood, 1880), p. 39.

pletely grasp its meaning.[37] Science could not understand what religion could, that nature meant little except what it signified about man and his attempt to reach God. Man rose above nature and subjected it to himself; but in the end the factor of self-love, implanted by nature, remained to combine with universal love for man's full freedom.

When man came out from under the dominance of nature or physical need, society was responsible. Men combining to subdue physical desires by greater production of material goods, James called society.[38] He assumed that their mutual efforts were dictated by charitable love, the foundation stone of society.[39] Men may have been selfish, but society demonstrated the first instance of altruism. Nature lost its power to cause men to feel they were independent, when man learned he could gain more physical security by cooperating with other men.

James never defined society clearly. Stephen Pearl Andrews, in a debate with James over marriage, accused James, quite legitimately, of confusing society and the state by not defining either clearly and by making the two interchangeable.[40] When James spoke of society, he meant the accumulation of formal and informal societal restrictions. Society could thus be any social institution or any commonly recognized moral sanction, since morality and society were, for James, two aspects of the same proposition.

One of the difficulties with the restrictions placed upon man by society was the possibility of clash between the law of society and the law of the individual's ideal action. James never hesitated in asserting his position, which was that social sanctions were inferior to ideal action, since ideal action came from God and social sanctions came from man. If society assumed the prerogative of contradicting ideal action, society transcended its purpose and must either be changed immediately or else lose the respect of mankind.[41] This was an extremely radical anarchical position, although some of the Transcendentalists might have had a similar view. Thoreau, in particular, might have agreed with James, except that Thoreau appealed to a moral law higher than the law of the state, rather than to a law of ideal action against that moral law.

[37] Henry James, *Society the Redeemed Form of Man,* p. 148.
[38] Henry James, *Lectures and Miscellanies,* p. 68.
[39] Henry James, *Moralism and Christianity,* p. 103.
[40] Stephen Pearl Andrews, *Love, Marriage and Divorce* (New York: Stringer and Townsend, 1853), p. 79.
[41] Henry James, *Lectures and Miscellanies,* pp. 40-41.

Because of the time lag always present between ideas and their institutional incorporation, the question of conflict between the two would seem permanent and insoluble. From the nature of this conflict between inspired action and societal regulation James formulated a law of social progress, one quite similar to individual growth. Institutions originated in man's inspired activity. By a dialectical process, institutions which were started for well-intentioned reasons ended up perverted. James explained the reason for institutional perversion by quoting the Biblical warning of what would happen when the letter of the law was supreme and the spirit was dead.[42]

One of the reasons why James is difficult to understand is that he frequently uses the same word to signify different concepts. Technically, James preferred not to use the word "society" to apply to existing institutions, laws, and group activities. "Society" or "socialism" should be reserved for the perfected fellowship which will exist in the future,[43] while the present life should be called "civilization."[44] After having made this distinction, James proceeds to call present institutional forms "society." James's definition of existing institutions as civilization reflects the influence that Fourier's ideas and vocabulary had on him. Society and civilization have been regarded as synonymous for purposes of clarity in this work, and the future society has been called the ideal society.

Society, like nature, had a dual function, negative and positive. One of the most dangerous problems rising out of the negative aspect of society was concerned with the development of a selfhood far beyond that established by the natural wants of man. Education, political institutions, and the family all contributed to an increased sense of independence.[45] Too often, man's elevated position in society inclined him to think himself superior; the family relationship especially nourished this sentiment.

It was for this reason that James attacked "the rage for multiplying schools and colleges" in the United States, for these reflected private instead of public interests.[46] One might suppose that had the schools taught more community concern and emphasized common unity in place of individual competition and achievement, James would have considered them more kindly. James objected

---

[42] Henry James, *The Secret of Swedenborg*, p. 72.
[43] Henry James, *The Church of Christ Not an Ecclesiasticism*, pp. 96-97.
[44] Austin Warren, *The Elder Henry James*, p. 210.
[45] Henry James, "Socialism and Civilization," p. 106.
[46] Mrs. John T. Sargent, p. 38.

not so much to the institutions themselves as to their wrong emphasis.

In many ways, however, the entire existing social framework was for James based upon false ideas and actually prevented men from achieving a more spontaneous life. Society, by the very fact that it was called into existence to satisfy physical needs, forced men to devote their entire energy to the satisfactions of these needs and to ignore their other, more spiritual, needs.[47] One of the major crimes of society against human nature resulted from the concentrating upon the controlled segment of man's life, which society fosters, to the exclusion of the creative portion. The complaint against the restrictive and stultifying nature of society was one with which the contemporary romantics could have sympathized. Thoreau, especially, would have agreed that the need to simplify was always present and that simplifications could best occur outside the confines of society.

This was not the worst of the matter. Society restricted the divine life in man by dividing man from God. The presumption of society that caused the divisive feeling was that the will of society was the will of God. James cited as an example the attempt of society to make property sacred by maintaining that God had originally condoned property sanctions, and hence the popular assumption that a violator of property rights outraged God.[48] To James, this was ridiculous. In addition to sinning, society tried to cover up sin by asserting that its laws were mere reflections of the laws of God. The concept of natural law was wrong, James supposed, largely because men used it as a rationalization of the laws which they already possessed. What had happened was that society was trying to sanctify its laws in order to make them stronger.

Society, man's collective institutions, did, however, contribute several ideas important for the education of man. Since society mirrored the needs and desires of men, men's hearts rather than their heads produced the instinct of social consciousness.[49] The community that this instinct developed superseded the original community set up to satisfy physical needs. This community could be identified by the common involvement of its members in moral decisions.[50] Society proved men capable of living under the law, and this ability to live in peace under law would be extended in the perfect society, so that the law could be removed with no

---

[47] Henry James, "Socialism and Civilization," p. 63.
[48] *Ibid.*, p. 65.
[49] Henry James, "Faith and Science," p. 374.
[50] Henry James, "The Radical Dogmatics," p. 85.

unfortunate results. In order to facilitate man's progress, the institutions which restrict man grow more universal as history progresses. Men proceed from the dominion of family up through the republic,[51] as society became increasingly inclusive.

Another contribution which society made toward the recognition of a more perfect fellowship was its tendency to reduce the men under its institutional control to a mean.[52] The growth of a median man may have disturbed James personally, but the growing indifference of society to the claims of the extremities in it proved that unitary man was coming. The leveling down and filling up done by institutional forces presaged the new society.

Yet James maintained conversely that society should not destroy genius, for the genius furthered society. While expressing pleasure at the leveling action of society, James also held with equal vigor that society secretly admired men who flouted its law in the interest of its own free activity. This was proved, James said, by the fact that no genius ever disdained society without society becoming reconciled to that individual and even honoring him.[53]

In spite of the fact that society heralded the new age that was sure to come, it was self-defeating. This was true because all ties, natural and social, led to slavery. Even the easiest social tie, the family, could be too restrictive. "I love my father and mother, my brother and sister, but I deny their unconditional property in me. . . . I will be the property of no person," said James.[54] Since all social ties resulted in slavery, society, in the end, must disappear. As James wrote to Emerson:

> Let the old imposter society go, bag and baggage, for a very real and substantial one is aching to come in, in which the churl shall not be exalted to a place of dignity, in which innocence shall never be tarnished or trafficked in, in which every man's freedom shall be respected down to its feeblest filament as the radiant altar of God.[55]

The thinking habits of James were somewhat peculiar. Ralph Barton Perry holds that, for James, "As soon as ideas became established, or were proclaimed with unction and airs of authority, they became repugnant. You could spoil any good thing for

[51] Mrs. John T. Sargent, p. 40.
[52] Henry James, *Lectures and Miscellanies*, p. 133.
[53] Henry James, *Moralism and Christianity*, p. 52.
[54] *Ibid.*, p. 87.
[55] Edward W. Emerson, *The Early Years of the Saturday Club* (Boston: Houghton Mifflin, 1918), p. 332.

him by converting it into an institution."[56] While this is probably too simple an explanation, it contains, nonetheless, a certain amount of truth.

Religion began in man with a sense of separation from God and a dissatisfaction with present life.[57] Basically, this constituted natural religion,[58] for each man, no matter where he lived, felt the need to gain an intimate connection with his gods. The desire to return to God inhered in all men.

James opposed natural religion as having a deeply mistaken concept of God, for the essence of the religious urge was the sense of the disparity of God and man, a sense the validity of which James denied. Men and God were intimately tied together. Deism, one of the facets of natural religion, compared God with a clockmaker, who wound up the universe and let it run. The impersonal relationship which a clockmaker had to his clocks revolted James enough so that he predicted other people would have the same reaction and would never make Deism popular.[59] Natural religion, however, was a more prevalent concept than Deism, for it appeared in many other religions of the world as well as in large segments of the Christian church.

Natural religion indicated a desirable instinct, one which was necessary to start men toward a reconciliation with God and which prompted the building of altars, the making of sacrifices, and the setting up of all the institutional forms[60] known to religion. Originally, the function of the church was to calm men's disquiet by pointing the way to God. The need for a more formal recognition of man's reconciliation with God prompted the creation of churches, whose institutional forms symbolized this reconciliation.

James nowhere denied that the church was important as an historical institution, for it had performed two absolutely necessary tasks. First, the formal Christian organization convinced many people of the veracity of the Christian facts. As the living witness to the truth of Christ's mission, the church claimed man's respect.[61] And second, every shred of spiritual truth that man possessed was given him by the church, which had among other virtues the distinction of first condemning selfishness and worldliness.[62]

[56] Perry, *The Thought and Character of William James*, p. 142.
[57] Henry James, *Substance and Shadow*, p. 221.
[58] *Ibid.*, p. 5.
[59] Henry James, Review of Foster's translation of *The True Christian Religion*, *Atlantic Monthly*, XXIII (1869), 766.
[60] Henry James, *The Secret of Swedenborg*, p. 73.
[61] Henry James, *Society the Redeemed Form of Man*, p. 292.
[62] *Ibid.*, p. 205.

However, the institutional product of man's religious instinct did not necessarily remain good, for, like nature, the church reflected the state of the culture in which it was found: "It has been animated by the average moral enlightenment of the time, and it had grown with men's moral growth."[63] As time passed, the church changed, sometimes for better and sometimes for worse. James never forgot that the church was man-made and that as such it participated in the life of its age.

Evil, however, overtook the church, as it overtook all institutions, religious as well as secular. In the church this was signalized by the gradually growing assumption that the religious aims of the institution and of man were identical.[64] In other words, the church came to assume that it deserved to be the final goal of religious instinct, rather than merely the means to satisfy religious instinct. The church believed its rules and doctrines epitomized the will of God and that the welfare of its institutional form was all-important. James, however, along with many other Protestants, believed that man could achieve direct connection with God[65] and that the church was only an instrument to facilitate the connection.

Given this goal, the church frustrated direct connection with God by interposing itself between man and God.[66] The institution which had started with the high ideal of satisfying man's needs and which had been successful, now refused to give up and insisted that its temporary function should be extended into a permanent one. By insisting that it had an intrinsic value, the church impeded the union of God with man. This was truly unfortunate, for the church had made the most pretensions to be identified with God and was, to the extent of these pretensions, far more harmful when perverted than less pretentious institutions.[67]

When the church became concerned with itself, it became as much a force for evil as it had been a force for good: "Professional religion . . . is the devil's masterpiece for ensnaring silly, selfish men."[68] Both extremes of contemporary, organized religion merited James's criticism; for ritualism was as damaging as its counter-

---

[63] Henry James, Review of Lee's *A History of Sacerdotal Celibacy in the Christian Church*, XX (1867), 379.

[64] Henry James, *The Church of Christ Not an Ecclesiasticism*, p. 45.

[65] Henry James, *Lectures and Miscellanies*, p. 202.

[66] Grattan, *The Three Jameses*, pp. 68-69.

[67] Henry James, *Society the Redeemed Form of Man*, p. 426.

[68] *Ibid.*, p. 42.

part, revivalism.[69] Ritualism caused men to be concerned with form rather than content; and revivalism, by emphasizing the terrible wrath of God, devoted too much time to man's selfish, personal hopes. James grew to hate the present, visible church; he went so far as to say that he regarded "the church's heartiest malison as God's heartiest benison...."[70]

Among the many ways the church subverted men was by forcing upon them an erroneous concept of the good life. The church directed man's attention to the next world, while ignoring the needs of this world. In order for man to gain salvation, according to the church, he had to drastically restrict the wants of the flesh, seeking to weaken the forces of the world as they interacted with his appetites. Therefore, celibacy was a higher good than marriage, although it was better to marry than to burn. James attacked the church's view by denying that man's primary concern should be the next world; for, as he constantly indicated, the world was good and physical wants were desirable. Since all life was eminently good, James believed in elevating practical, everyday life.[71]

An even graver temptation than asceticism faced the visible church. Starting from a living record of man's universal need, despair, and poverty, the church evolved into a "flattering witness of our private wealth, of our strictly individual assurance or presumption."[72] The church's function was not to flatter men; the church was supposed to be a witness to man's sin and inadequacy and to aid the union of man and God. The tendency to make the church a record of man's moral achievement instead of his sin was, said James, precisely what Jesus had fought in the church of His time.[73] The only enemy Christ had was the Pharisee, who attributed righteousness to himself and iniquity to others. Christ taught that all men were on amicable terms with God, with no one having personal merit or demerit in His eyes. The Christian church had originally followed Christ's ideas; but all too soon, it reverted to the exclusive righteousness of the Jewish church.

Thus, in the final analysis the church became the cause and very center of spiritual sin; it fostered a belief in every man that he was nearer to God than another.[74] James evaluated the church-

---

[69] *Ibid.*
[70] William James, p. 93.
[71] Henry James, *Substance and Shadow*, p. 209.
[72] *Ibid.*, p. 23.
[73] Henry James, *The Secret of Swedenborg*, p. 83.
[74] Henry James, *Society the Redeemed Form of Man*, p. 200.

goer and decided that he had many undesirable qualities, one of which was to gain every eternal mark of God's favor that the church could give. If the church fulfilled its duty by scourging its members and proclaiming them to be total sinners, they would withdraw from the church, allowing it to fend for itself.[75] Most church members displayed hearts so cold that they would contribute no effort to save another human being from sin or punishment, while at the same time maintaining an outward devoutness so overdone that it nauseated James.[76]

The men representing the church were not better than the degraded institutional form. Ministers and priests may have started with perfectly good intentions and very respectable intellectual abilities. But all too soon they became professionals, losing their souls to an institution, regarding the form embodied in the pulpit as sacred, and becoming incapable of any really individual action.[77] James's strictures against members of the clergy were on a par with his opinions of church members.

If priests claimed to be representatives of God on earth, they should act as if they were. A true minister of God would attempt to bring about the perfect society and to eliminate ignorance, licentiousness, intemperance, waste, and contention between men. While James insisted that congregations should demand that their ministers be reformers,[78] he doubted that this would be effective, since most of the priests could not even see man's suffering. Those few who were able to see man's plight often refused to discuss methods of alleviation, for they held it to be a sin to attempt to change the world.[79] James voiced a criticism here similar to that which social gospel ministers made some decades later. It is interesting to compare James's indictment of the clergy with his attitude toward reformers. Most reformers demonstrated deep spiritual sin, thought James, for they were most often impressed with their own moral rectitude and solicitous of the morals of others, with the intention of improving these morals so that they would correspond with the reformer's own.[80] No more specific definition of moral selfhood need be made. Yet James had the temerity to suggest that ministers become reformers. One must

---

[75] Henry James, *Substance and Shadow*, p. 192.
[76] *Ibid.*, p. 218.
[77] Warren, p. 24.
[78] Henry James, *Lectures and Miscellanies*, p. 313.
[79] *Ibid.*, p. 312.
[80] Henry James, *The Nature of Evil*, p. 331.

assume that James hoped that these ministers would not be plagued with a self-righteous moral sense.

When James studied the historic forms manifested by the church, he reached some interesting conclusions. The Roman Catholic Church was a product of Christ's dispensation, succeeding the Jewish church which had erred in assuming that the moral difference in men was actual. As we have seen, however, the Catholic Church soon lapsed into the same error, which time compounded. James disclosed his own attitude toward the Catholic organization when he attacked the worship of saints; he supposed that "the Romish church unquestionably deals with a lower order of heart and mind than the Protestant does, and is very apt to breed therefore much more coarse and brutal conceptions of sanctity when it breeds any."[81]

The Catholic church committed a second great error when it interposed the body of the church between man and God by inaugurating a separate and distinctive priesthood. The institution of a distinctive priestly order led to the danger of sinful priests, for the temptation to regard themselves as spriritually superior to other church members was very great. Yet, James thought, despite this and other difficulties, the Catholic church did a great deal of good for its own time within its rather restricted framework.[82]

The Protestant churches evolved from the Catholic, the relation between the two resembling that of the stem to the root. Because of this close relationship between the two faiths, trouble was bound to occur.[83] However, the evolution of the Protestant branch was logical and necessary, leading to a better society. The most important difference between the old and new faith, and therefore the one that most sharply separated them, was that the Protestant faith caused secular elements to intermingle with religious ones, while the Catholic faith had remained purely religious.

This meant that Protestants distinguished less between the practical and the religious life, making them the same. The priesthood vanished as a distinctive order, and ministers were ordained who participated in other social institutions, including marriage. Protestantism also tended to make every man a priest and improved on Catholicism by denying that man could contribute any important help toward his own salvation, as workers were subordinated to faith and God's grace. The two improvements fostered by

---

[81] Henry James, *Society the Redeemed Form of Man,* p. 441.
[82] Henry James, *The Nature of Evil,* pp. 165-66.
[83] Henry James, *Substance and Shadow,* p. 211.

Protestantism were these: (1) an emphasis upon man's direct connection with God and a de-emphasis on the church; and (2) a universalizing of the priesthood and religion by a combination with secular life and institutions.[84]

Protestantism was the best institutional religious form that man had known, not because it was the final form but because it pointed to the final form that would assure complete spiritual freedom for the individual.[85] Yet even the Protestant organization revealed several weaknesses to James's critical eye. Calvinism, logically enough, was rejected by James with hearty good will,[86] for it was far too exclusive for his tastes. Then too, James disapproved of the rapid proliferation of sects within Protestantism, which was but another aspect of Protestant exclusiveness. The Catholic church, despite its many faults, at least had the virtue of universal pretension, while those congregations afflicted with the sectarian temper were of an entirely different stamp, elevating exclusiveness over every other virtue.[87]

The sectarian temper could be found among many churches; the distinguishing attitude was an air of superiority over other people. This was often combined with an erroneous conception of the church, for sectarians preferred to define the church, as the Catholics had, as a visible corporation that furnished the sole means to salvation. James maintained that the only consistent exponent of the church's monopoly on salvation was the Catholic church.[88] If sectarians wished to be consistent, they should recognize the prior claims of the Roman church and either discard their sectarian temper or return to the Catholic church.

Besides these aberrations, the Protestant spirit was quite susceptible to temptation and subsequent perversion; and since the Protestant niche was higher than the Catholic, the inclination to fall was greater, even to the point of being overwhelming. Protestantism had erred in making redemption and salvation the same, thus differentiating between the individual and the race.[89] This was derivative from the larger error that assumed Christ's sacrifice was insufficient for all.[90] These two errors hinted at the major difficulty in Protestant thought. Although the Protestant spirit

[84] Henry James, *The Nature of Evil,* pp. 166-67.
[85] Henry James, *The Church of Christ Not an Ecclesiasticism,* p. 87.
[86] Perry, *The Thought and Character of William James,* pp. 14-15.
[87] Henry James, *The Church of Christ Not an Ecclesiasticism,* pp. 27-28.
[88] *Ibid.,* pp. 33-34.
[89] Henry James, *The Nature of Evil,* p. 166.
[90] *Ibid.,* p. 171.

declared for freedom, this freedom might be perverted to personal rather than universal ends. Protestantism had made all men priests, so now all men were subject to the same danger that only the Catholic priesthood had faced before.

What has been suggested before can now be stated directly. Protestantism, whose relation to religion was the equivalent of democracy's relation to government, was not an expansion of the old Catholic organization in the direction of a bigger and better institutional form, but an actual disorganization of this form. "They — Protestantism and democracy — mark the old age of those institutions Church and state, their decline into the vale of years, preparatory to their final exit from the historic scene."[91] Protestantism characterized institutional evolution in that it set up no new, elaborate institutional form, indicating instead the disintegration of the old, arbitrary Catholic form.

Protestantism, however, did not stop there. James anticipated that the church, which served to introduce the state, would merge with the state and disappear as a separate entity.[92] He thought that he could see this happening in the society of his day and was pleased with this indication of progress toward the good society. The church and state possessed two distinct functions, one of which followed the other in a complementary fashion. The church pictured man's sense of humbleness and unworthiness, while the state initiated man's return to a lofty position by giving him dominion over the earth.[93]

James never distinguished clearly between society and the state, assuming, for all practical purposes, that they were identical. After reviewing the history of social forms, he took a familiar position as to their evolution. Marriage was first, followed by the family, the tribe, the town, and the nation, in that order.[94] Sometimes James included the commune form between the tribe and the town and appended the empire and the republic after the nation. The commune resembled the Greek city state, and the empire and republic were composed of many units immediately smaller.[95] Each of these "experiences," as James preferred to call them, was social as well as political, progressing from the most particular and simple to the most universal and complex. Man learned how to become a social creature under the tutelage of ever larger

91 Henry James, *Christianity the Logic of Creation*, p. 208.
92 Henry James, *The Church of Christ Not an Ecclesiasticism*, pp. 79-80.
93 *Ibid.*, p. 64.
94 Henry James, *Moralism and Christianity*, p. 110.
95 Henry James, "Spiritual Creation," p. 134.

institutional forms. In his ideas on the development of political entities, James displayed some tinge of evolutionary thinking.

The first educative institution possessed by man was marriage, which James regarded as one of the most perfectly devised institutions. Marriage forced man to neglect his physical strength and control in favor of social persuasion. The lesson in socialization taught by marriage could never have been learned elsewhere.[96] However, like any other social institution, marriage depended upon the use that it had for its value. Marriage might be designed for a high goal and yet be perverted and misused, just as any institution could be.[97] That had happened to the marriage institution in his own day, James concluded, for it had lost its flexibility and had become bound by tradition. This was bad, since the past should not determine customs so much as the needs of the present.

It was in defense of the flexibility of the marriage institution that James argued against Horace Greeley for the necessity of divorce, even at the risk of being called an advocate of free love. James contended "that it was not essential to the honor of marriage that the persons should be compelled to live together when they held the reciprocal relation of dog and cat. . . ."[98] Marriage customs should never be so rigid as to deny that mistakes could happen and to provide no means for rectifying those mistakes.

Since formal marriage was strictly a social institution growing out of the needs of human culture rather than human nature, and since ideal marriage was a symbolic blending of natural man, male, with spiritual man, female,[99] the institution was certain to evolve into an ideal form. By James's dialectic this was accomplished by a process of institutional decay. James indicated that decay was evident because of the more liberal divorce legislation of the day, which was not cause for alarm, but signalized progress to the good society.[100]

Institutionally speaking, marriage was losing its absolute position. James conceived that the loss of the legal or "ritual" sanctity of marriage actually heralded a gain in true sanctity; for James never doubted that if the protection afforded by law were removed the next day, almost all married people would remain married and

[96] Sargent, p. 209.
[97] Andrews, p. 26.
[98] *Ibid.*, p. 25.
[99] Henry James, "The Woman Thou Gavest Me," *Atlantic Monthly,* XXV (1870), 66.
[100] *Ibid.*, p. 70.

devoted to each other.[101] The monogamous union of man and woman was the result of a spontaneous urge residing deep within the nature of the participants and needed no legal action to uphold it.

The important truth in marriage was the inner urge, which had to be developed to nurture social institutions and without which these institutions would immediately disintegrate.[102] Marriage had, in turn, produced family life, the primary cell upon which society was based,[103] for the family expanded the social aspects of the marriage relationship to include children. The family symbolized the new society, where all men were brothers. Too often, however, the family head substituted coercion instead of cooperative love to hold the family together.[104] James scorned this perversion in the family but conceded that it was as typical of family life as of society.

The family, like the formal marriage institution, will disappear as a legal entity, leaving only the bonds of love to bind it still. However, until the ideal society comes the legal restrictions maintaining the family will be important. Home was a place of refuge for man, where he could develop spontaneously, free from the dead hand of institutional life.[105] One notes that James reflects the patriarchal organization of his day, in that only the head of the household benefitted from this sanctuary.

The expanding social controls that were initiated by the family became final in the state, which represented all of the organized groups using compulsion within the geographic limits.[106] Harmonizing these diverse compulsions by the addition of its own, the state reflected the condition of man in his own particular age and culture, the disharmony in the state merely mirroring the disharmony in man.[107]

Within the state itself, several institutions gained the blessings of society through the agency of the state. Property, for example, was good in that it showed that man was conquering and possessing

---

[101] Andrews, *Love, Marriage, and Divorce*, pp. 25-26.

[102] Henry James, "The Logic of Marriage and Murder," *Atlantic Monthly*, XXV (1870), 745.

[103] Henry James, "Is Marriage Holy?" p. 364.

[104] From Stephen Dewhurst's *Autobiography*, quoted in Matthiessen, *The James Family*, p. 31.

[105] Henry James, "Woman and the Woman's Movement," p. 284.

[106] Henry James, Review of Clark's *The Question of the Hour*, *Atlantic Monthly*, XXV (1870), 638-39.

[107] Henry James, "The Social Significance of Our Institutions," in Joseph Blau, p. 250.

nature and thus asserting his individuality.[108] From the necessity of protecting, police and other coercive instruments of the state sprang. However, property had a more important symbolic value since it symbolized "the perfect sovereignty which man is destined to exercise over nature."[109] Man could learn about freedom and sovereignty over nature only by experience; this experience was afforded him by private property.

Unfortunately, man came to regard property less as symbolically meaningful and more as an end in itself, even as having meaning divorced from its utility and value as a source of pleasure.[110] The change never became complete, however, for men were ashamed — in direct ratio to their spiritual enlightenment — of the high position which they assigned property. In addition, spiritually enlightened men deprecated the limitation that private property placed upon freedom and sovereignty.[111]

James's view of property was not radical; rather it was quite similar to that of the Protestant scholastics, as they were called, who defended property for its use. Property, they maintained, originated to benefit man and to aid his moral sense. James would have heartily agreed with such a formulation.

In the interest of more freedom, however, James thought man should demand more property and not less: "Nature and society should have no power to identify me with a particular potato-patch and a particular family of mankind all my days. The fact of my divine genesis makes God's whole earth my home, makes all His children my intimates and brethren."[112] This was the kind of socialism that James wanted. He believed that all property should be available to every man, who would take only what he needed. No institutional form would be required, and no concrete plan for the achievement of the goal was necessary. Again, James assumed almost a perfect harmony among men, with each man satisfying only his necessary, physical needs.

Man's needs created governments just as they had created private property. Society had preached government, since government was instituted only as a means to organize and control society. The need for order and protection within society produced governments; these governments should, therefore, be sensi-

---

108 Henry James, *Lectures and Miscellanies*, pp. 25-26.
109 *Ibid.*, p. 63.
110 *Ibid.*, p. 55.
111 *Ibid.*, pp. 69-70.
112 Henry James, *Moralism and Christianity*, pp. 67-68.

tive to the needs of society and be flexible enough to adjust to social change.[113] In the very restricted sense that governments reflected social needs, they can be said to come from God and to testify to the new and harmonious society that was coming.[114]

Government served as an educational agency just as other organizations of society had. Education from government was negative in that it consisted of giving man outward discipline in social affairs under the coercive force of the law.[115] When the task of education was finished, governments will pass away. Since the main business of government was disciplinary, governors, by their very nature, qualified as authoritarians. Defined as such, the office of political headship would require only the lowest virtues of its occupants. A consideration of the matter convinced James that either General Jackson or Louis Napoleon, for whom James had no respect, were preferable as secular rulers to the mystic Fénelon and the Apostle John for whom James had the highest respect, since the governing of men was "the lowest of vocations."[116] The most spiritual individual had the least desire and qualifications for regulating citizens.

Following this line of reasoning would lead one to suppose that the most evil men, spiritually considered, would be the most qualified to rule. James would not agree with so extreme a statement, since there were limits below which no ruler should go. Louis Napoleon was preferable to the "crowned imbecilities" whom he replaced; James recognized several degrees of evil and wanted political rulers to possess the lowest one. As James said, Napoleon and Mazzini "became irresistibly precious and sweet to my heart, even as terriers and weasels are precious to the agriculturist long vexed by predatory and fugacious vermin. . . ."[117] The revolutions which these men symbolized revealed degenerate political institutions for what they were and thus were instruments of progress.

James studied the governments of his time and concluded that governmental progression had gone about as far as possible. The United States government, which James alternately described as a republic and as a democracy, exemplified the final institutional phase. Democracy was the last educative political institution man could conceive, because the institutionalizing of any more freedom

[113] Henry James, *The Nature of Evil*, pp. 96-97.
[114] Henry James, *Lectures and Miscellanies*, pp. 14-15.
[115] *Ibid.*, p. 38.
[116] Henry James, *Substance and Shadow*, p. 253.
[117] Henry James, *Christianity the Logic of Creation*, p. 182.

would have been impossible.[118] Although democracy was the best governmental form man had devised, it too must die. Human thought and action had been given wider range in democratic governments than in any other political society, the most binding restriction upon man being that of informal social humanity.[119] Given the choice of competing governmental forms, James would have selected democracy, as he viewed any society which used representative institutions as nearer the final recognition of man's involuntary brotherhood with man than a society which did not.

Democracy, which James categorized as the secular heir of Protestantism, showed few positive political qualities. Originating as a revolutionary movement, democracy denied established institutions and affirmed the sovereignty of the people. Representative government also reduced authority to a bare minimum, with the exception of that necessary to promote the welfare of the whole people,[120] a small category for James. This meant that democracy was a disorganization of political life,[121] just as Protestantism was a disorganization of religious life. The old hierarchy of privilege and inequality would soon be completely overthrown.[122]

Just as the sign of a religious society was the strict adherence and maintenance of the moral law, so secular sanctions marked political society. The moral law required obedience and inspired good until men were capable of spiritual fellowship; then a continued existence became not only unnecessary but distinctly harmful. Similarly, the laws of the state, as promulgated and enforced by the government, upheld the good until man's training enabled him to act spontaneously; but then these laws should not stand in the way of man's inherent freedom. Both moral and secular law, in order to remain untainted, should work for the race, and the race should work for man. Most of the trouble engendered by secular and religious law resulted when law rejected or ignored this eternal principle.[123]

Proper laws displayed no personal or divided interests but insisted instead on the universal interests of man. Operating from this premise, James attacked the marriage laws of his time, for these laws reflected a limited, rather than a universal, concern for

---

[118] Henry James, *Society the Redeemed Form of Man*, p. 306.

[119] Henry James, *The Church of Christ Not an Ecclesiasticism*, pp. 87-88.

[120] Henry James, *Lectures and Miscellanies*, pp. 2-4.

[121] Henry James, quoted in Grattan, p. 67.

[122] Henry James, "Woman and the Woman's Movement," p. 279.

[123] Stephen Dewhurst's *Autobiography*, quoted in Matthiessen, *The James Family*, p. 21.

man.[124] Secular law, in general, did not reveal a concern for the welfare of all men; it did not ensure equal justice and mercy to all. Responsibility for the crime and evil in social life must be partially shared by society,[125] and its leaders;[126] for if the law protects when men are starving, those who make and support the law encourage stealing.

According to James, man was powerless either to keep or to break the law. He explained his curious idea in this fashion: if man saw that the law and his own physical and social needs coincided, then he would, in no circumstances, break that law, since that action would be contrary to his own interests (James, as we have seen, assumed that no man would ever act against his own interests); but if the law and physical or social needs disagreed, the power of these needs drives man to break the law.[127] In either case man cannot be said to be acting in a free manner; he was determined, and so no credit or blame ought to be assessed. Also, the very fact that secular law could be broken furnished proof that the law was of natural and not of divine origin, since one of the tenets of divine law was harmony within itself.

Vice and crime, then, symbolized the wrong restrictions that nature and society had placed upon man, and not man's evil nature. James even insisted that men involved in acts of vice and crime reveal man's divine nature, for vice represents an attempt by man to realize his ideas in action without the consent of nature, and crime represents an attempt to act ideally without the approval of society.[128] James did not condone these practices but found hope in them, since they typified man's struggle to act freely. The body was destroyed by vice, and society punished crime, and thus these actions were self-defeating and earned their own punishment.[129]

The liars, thieves, murderers, and adulterers in society performed two important functions. First, they prevented an all-inclusive social tyranny by striking at the laws of society; second, they hinted at the freer society to come. The disorganization of law showed the movement to freedom as much as the disorganization of religion. Criminals pointed the way to the good society.

---

[124] Henry James, "Is Marriage Holy?" p. 365.

[125] Henry James, *Lectures and Miscellanies*, pp. 21-23.

[126] *Ibid.*, p. 374.

[127] Henry James, Review of J. C. Shairp's *Culture and Religion in Some of Their Relations, Atlantic Monthly*, XXVIII (1871), 253.

[128] Henry James, *Lectures and Miscellanies*, p. 349.

[129] Henry James, *Moralism and Christianity*, p. 46.

As for the criminals themselves, James always retained the optimistic view that the assumption of the burden of guilt by society would reform these criminals. One example discussed by James was the drunkard. If society magnanimously opened its arms to him and said that the responsibility for his drunkenness was on its shoulders for having failed to provide suitable outlets for his ideal action, the drunkard would "put on vigor and beauty with the day; and shed the slough of natural habit as spontaneously as flowers shed their foliage, or corn its husks."[130]

James, as a socialist, believed that man in his majority was sufficient in himself and that no outward social control in the form of informed social sanctions, religious ordinances, or governmental law was necessary.[131] The most radically free institutions, Protestantism and Democracy, will pass away, and the new church and the new society will be an invisible entity held together by love.[132]

James never faltered in his belief that definite progress toward the goal of perfect human freedom and fellowship existed. Progress might be slow and gradual, as man must recognize variety before unity becomes plain,[133] but progress never stopped. All history pointed to the onward and upward rise of the race of man in whom progress inhered. Any man now living was nearer true fellowship and the perfect society than his ancestors simply because of the educative process men had undergone throughout their history.[134]

Faith in the progress of human nature to its final perfection enabled James to find hope in every event that transpired. Evil might seem dominant in the world, proven by the perfidy of men in the offices of church and state and in the low regard for the marriage vow,[135] and yet this did not mean that progress was impeded. On the contrary, one of the necessary steps involved in progress entailed the destruction of institutional forms; might not this obvious evil indicate that these forms were destroying themselves? On the credit side, arbitrary governments were being overthrown by revolutionary fervor; this was also due to the rise

---

130 Henry James, *Lectures and Miscellanies*, pp. 431-32.
131 Matthiessen, *The James Family*, p. 50.
132 Henry James, "Swedenborg's Ontology," *North American Review*, CV (1867), 121.
133 Henry James, *Moralism and Christianity*, p. 109.
134 Henry James, *Christianity the Logic of Creation*, pp. 172-73, note.
135 William James, p. 313.

of the spirit of freedom and fellowship in man.[136] The growth of volunteer societies pleased James, for the Temperance Cause, the Anti-slavery Movement, and the societies for redeeming sinners and alleviating the pangs of poverty, were evidence that men were changing for the better.[137] One notes that progress occurs despite the efforts of good or evil men and that all persons and events contribute to progress.

It would be extremely difficult to postulate a more all-embracing view of progress, where every event was conducive to favorable growth. The death of arbitrary governments and the growth of more representative ones, combined with the perversion of social institutions and the existence of evil men in society, all pointed to progress. James stated that man, educated by nature and society, could at last dispense with these disciplinary organizations in favor of a voluntary society. Perhaps the great difference between James's view of progress and those of other romantics was that when James indicated that history was the march of freedom through the world, he meant just that. Belief in progress was an article of faith for James, as it made possible his belief in a beneficent God.[138]

---

[136] Andrews, p. 60.
[137] Henry James, *The Nature of Evil*, pp. 329-31.
[138] Henry James, *Society the Redeemed Form of Man*, p. 12.

Six

Consequences

With the previous chapter's discussion of James's attitudes toward society in mind, let us proceed to examine his theories for their interpretation and application. Grattan, in his book on *The Three Jameses,* maintains that the elder James paid little or no attention to the expanding seams of American life but was completely engaged in building an ideal construct.[1] But this is an overstatement, for James took the opportunity to mention many events that happened during his life to illustrate and prove his ideas.

Van Wyck Brooks, to the contrary, declares that James was a proud American. Brooks holds that James believed that "American life was a quicksand in which everything held most dear was in peril of being engulfed and lost,"[2] compelling James to take his five children to Europe to escape this fate. Stressing this thesis, Brooks could trace a more solid background for the younger Henry James, who lived as an expatriate, but in doing so, he paints an unfair picture of the elder Henry James.

James never denied that many ideas and institutions of America were not only unnecessary but even evil. The American church was not performing adequately, since individualism, recklessly selfish, had come to abide in its altars. Questions of reform were refused consideration; some ministers attacked those who brought up these questions for attempting to put through programs that would detract from the religious nature of the church.[3]

There were, however, more obvious evils in America than the

---

[1] Grattan, *The Three Jameses,* p. 54.

[2] Van Wyck Brooks, *The Pilgrimage of Henry James* (New York: E. P. Dutton, 1925), pp. 17-18.

[3] Warren, *The Elder Henry James,* p. 81.

low condition of churches and piety. The outstanding problem, which pressed upon everyone, was what to do about slavery. James's position on slavery was not a radical one; in fact, it coincided with that of most Northerners. As late as July 4, 1861, twenty days after the start of the Civil War, James maintained that although slavery was "an unmitigated infamy," the only recourse a citizen had was to prevent the extension of slavery into the territories and to persuade slave owners to voluntarily liberate their slaves.[4] Lincoln and the Republican Party had won on a similar program.

Those who attacked the institution of slavery where it already existed, in state or territory, interested James. He respected their upright and just approach to the problem of slavery, especially when compared to the attitude of those who attacked them; but he thought the abolitionist theory was difficult to justify. The abolitionist viewed slavery as a moral wrong done to the slaves by their master; this position, in turn, alienated the slaveholder by making him seem morally reprehensible. James favored regarding slavery as a spiritual sin, apart from the institution itself, injuring the master far more than the slave. The slaveholder was in greater mortal danger because he was much less able to regard all men as brothers and to visualize himself as a dependent creature. James assumed that the revelation of this truth to the slaveholder would be received with good will.[5] One wonders how valid his opinion was; one wonders whether a concern for the soul of the master might not be infinitely more irritating than an attack on the morality of the institution. In any event, James viewed slavery with a traditional Christian concern and believed that the institution was a very black mark on American society.

The problem of defalcation caused James more concern than the existence of evil institutions in America, since institutions were destined for an evil end anyway. Particularly noticeable was the low level of individual ability and honesty in political life. Jefferson Davis and James Buchanan typified the low estate of political society for James, as the ostentation and luxury of nonpolitical society heralded the degeneracy of that society.[6] However, James found hope in his belief that corruption was a scourge sent by God to hasten the birth of a new society. James's peculiar conception

---

[4] Henry James, "The Social Significance of Our Institutions," quoted in Blau, p. 254.
[5] Henry James, *Substance and Shadow*, p. 536, note.
[6] *Ibid.*, p. 13.

of progress enabled him to criticize American society and yet to be optimistic about the future.

Regardless of the many faults of America, it was, James thought, still far in advance of the Old World, which retained the idea that man's destiny was primarily concerned with the life to be enjoyed in the next world rather than with the present life. America, due to a lucky combination of democratic institutions and Protestant ideals, believed in the redemption of man on a practical, secular plane.[7] The geographical isolation that the United States enjoyed aided in the advance of the spiritual level, for Americans were insulated from the vicious institutions of Europe, both secular and sacerdotal, by the Atlantic Ocean.[8]

The differences between the American and European spirits, however, signified more than institutional differences, for ideological separation created these institutional differences. James decided that the essence of the American spirit was contained within the Declaration of Independence, which asserted, with sentiment closely akin to religious affirmation, that men were "created equal" and which supposed a social brotherhood based upon this statement.[9] Democratic life in America, as it was but imperfectly seen, nonetheless revealed the underlying equalitarian ideal.

Americans, acting upon the premise of equality and subsequent brotherhood that they inherited from the founding fathers, respected no institution, believing institutions had no value except for their usefulness to man. No part of government was to be maintained if the people wished to abolish it. Suppose, James speculated, the citizens of the United States decided that the presidency was an obsolete office, deserving to have its functions transferred to the Senate; this would be permissible. Going even further and abolishing the Senate in favor of the House of Representatives was not wrong if the people so desired.[10] (This was in 1852, some fifteen years before the fight between Congress and the President over reconstruction policies.) No political or social institution was so sacrosanct that the American public could not change or reject it.

James gloried in the iconoclastic attitude of Americans toward institutions; and although all history functioned as an educative experience, James thought the American past the most educative

7 William James, ed., *The Literary Remains of Henry James*, p. 370.
8 Henry James, *Lectures and Miscellanies*, pp. 8-9.
9 *Ibid.*, pp. 94-95.
10 *Ibid.*, pp. 8-9.

of all, since it revealed the maximum of freedom. James felt this freedom deeply: "Thank God we know no past in this country, but are a virgin people fresh from the hand of infinite love, sent forth to achieve an unprecedented destiny by the unprecedented method of a complete reliance upon the heart of man."[11]

Ordinarily, belief in the divinely ordained mission of America was intimately connected with the faith that this mission was to transform the entire world, a faith which James shared. Americans love America, he maintained, because America invited all to come and partake of her liberty and not because of any exclusiveness in her democratic institutions.[12] James could not have been patriotic had America been a particular instead of a universal institution.

The critics of American society were wanting in perception, according to James. The people who were determined to redeem and renew society by eliminating the evil within it were not themselves spiritually good men.[13] Most reformers suffered from the delusion that because they were morally better than other men, a distinction indicating only the probability that these men were most fortunately situated to follow the laws of nature and society, they were then also spiritually better.

James did, however, admire Fourier, the Utopian Socialist. Fourier, in contrast to other reformers, displayed the qualities of a spiritually enlightened man. Fourier's piety was preeminent since it resisted the drift toward traditional piety, composed as it was of moralism and prompted by a selfish impulse to placate an angry God, and instead desired the happiness and enlightenment of all men.[14] The difference between Fourier and other reformers was the difference between a humble and a proud attitude.

But even starting with the proper attitude did not assure Fourier's correctness about the nature of society. All socialists, Fourier included, misconceived the fundamental reason for society, assuming, like the liberals, that society was a product of natural law operating in the universe. Consequently, a perfect institutional form was possible.[15] The perfect society, socialists thought, might have existed in the dim past, the "Golden Age" of the Greeks, or it might come in the far distant future, the classless society of Marx. But James denied that society, composed as it was of coer-

[11] *Ibid.*, pp. 94-95.

[12] Blau, ed., *American Philosophic Addresses*, p. 238.

[13] Henry James, *The Nature of Evil*, p. 331.

[14] Henry James, *Socialism and Civilization*, quoted in Matthiessen, *The James Family*, p. 58.

[15] Henry James, *The Church of Christ Not an Ecclesiasticism*, pp. 96-97.

cive elements, could ever be perfected. The best institutional form was no form; hence Proudhon, in James's estimation, was much nearer a true idea of the nature of society when he attacked it for contending that it reflected God. Proudhon, according to James, had used a truly Christian judgment in condemning institutions.[16]

In discussing institutional religions, James was equally vociferous. Two men, Reverend Lyman Beecher and Dr. Horace Bushnell, were singled out by James as typifying the two extremes of contemporary religious temper — the emotional and the reasoned approach to religious truth and experience. Regardless of the differing emphasis, however, the men arrived at the same conclusion. Beecher's instructions and practices made God "the supreme devil of the universe";[17] for God possessed all the undesirable spiritual qualities, in particular, extreme wrath and justice. Bushnell, conversely, attempted to elevate morality to a much higher plane by making morality part of the divine essence. His attempt divulged Manichean tendencies, since the Manichean error was the attribution of the origin of moral good to God and the attribution of moral evil to a similarly powerful source. Bushnell had created an "evil possibility" within the nature of God.[18] Both Bushnell and Beecher ended by worshipping a devilish God.

As James studied the contemporary religious field, he was struck by the many existing institutional forms. Among the proliferation of sects was the Swedenborgian, which believed in the literal truth in Swedenborg's writings. James regarded Swedenborg as having several virtues, among them the ability to grasp the large general principles behind phenomena, but these virtues did not include being a great original thinker. Since Swedenborg merely reported what God had given him, James accepted the necessity of interpreting Swedenborg's works with imaginative understanding.[19] James did not spare Swedenborg's lapses, an affront to Swedenborgians, nor did he consider Swedenborg as possessing any aesthetic or imaginative qualities.[20]

As can be readily gathered, James and the Swedenborgians had grounds for disagreement. The Swedenborgians elevated Swedenborg to the position of a prophet, while James continued to insist that their idol had feet of clay. More serious, however, was James's

16 Henry James, *Christianity the Logic of Creation,* p. 211.
17 William James, p. 354, note.
18 Henry James, *The Secret of Swedenborg,* p. 93.
19 Warren, *The Elder Henry James,* p. 63.
20 William Dean Howells, *Literary Friends and Acquaintances,* p. 267.

attack upon Swedenborgians in the name of Swedenborg. James maintained, with considerable evidence, that Swedenborg had never intended to create a new church. Had not Swedenborg supported the ordinances of the established church in Sweden and remained a member of that church? What Swedenborg had actually intended was not a new institution but a new spirit that would destroy all institutions.[21]

Institutionally speaking, the Swedenborgians had no reason for existence; but since they had organized, they could be used as the best example of the common sectarian mistake. This mistake occurred when an institution was formed and it consisted of placing the letter of the law above the spirit of the law. The Jewish church in Jesus' time had illustrated this error, and now the Swedenborgians multiplied the gross aberration. Culling his mind for a suitable symbol, James finally hit upon one that adequately described Swedenborgian preoccupation with the visible law. The Swedenborgians, James said, carried, in lieu of a head, a huge wen upon their shoulders, inscribed with the motto "sanctity of the word."[22]

The greatest heresy of the Swedenborgians was the sectarian spirit, and the essence of this spirit was the sense of spiritual superiority.[23] Although Swedenborg had spoken for a universal spirit of brotherhood, the Swedenborgians had become one of the most particular branches of a particular spirit. James maintained that he was the true Swedenborgian, since he believed in universal spiritual equality.

There was, in the end, a symbolic meaning to be derived from the great sectarian urge of the Swedenborgians, one which might be commensurable with the progress of society. In a letter to the editor of the *New Jerusalem Magazine,* the organ of the New Church of America, James recorded his opinion of the rapid spread of sectarian sentiment in the New Church: "The old sects are notoriously bad enough, but your sect compares with these very much as a heap of dried cod on Long Wharf in Boston compared with the same fish while enjoying the freedom of the Atlantic Ocean."[24] No better proof was necessary for James to conclude that his analysis of Protestantism as a disorganization of the church was correct.[25] Did not the Swedenborgians indicate that his dis-

---

[21] Henry James, *The Church of Christ Not an Ecclesiasticism,* p. 175.
[22] William James, p. 368.
[23] Henry James, *The Church of Christ Not an Ecclesiasticism,* p. 33.
[24] Matthiessen, *The James Family,* pp. 105-06.
[25] Henry James, *The Church of Christ Not an Ecclesiasticism,* pp. 36-37.

organization was almost complete and that a new society was coming in?

Other religious institutions did not escape James's dissecting mind. Although the Unitarians had the only living theological doctrine in contemporary religious life,[26] they could profitably learn about sin from the Calvinists. Unitarianism, moreover, was a refuge for cultivated, intellectually oriented people who had only moral good and who worshipped God on the same aesthetic basis that they reverenced art and nature.[27] Objecting to this bloodless attitude, James declared that men should seek out religious satisfaction with the same passion they sought out physical and moral gratification. With this admonition, James dismissed the Unitarians.

The Universalists, whom James placed near the Unitarian theological position, had some erroneous ideas, including the doctrine of universal salvation, which James opposed in the name of free will for man.[28] God gave man free choice to go either to heaven or to hell, and even God ought not force a man into heaven against his own will. With that exception, however, James considered their errors as minor and praised the Universalists, as he had the Unitarians. Both Universalists and Unitarians modified the church into an almost completely secular institution and as a result of this secular temper promoted "kindly feeling and good manners."[29] Both these groups promoted the advent of the ideal fellowship.

Mormonism produced a violent reaction in James. He regarded Mormons as diabolic, illustrating with the Swedenborgians, the complete chaos of organized religion.[30]

Religious communitarians, however, presented a far more serious problem for James than did authoritarian movements. Authoritarian religious movements could be denounced with the seams and rifts in their thought uncovered; but religious groups which professed to allow religious impulses free play and which set up communities designed to further these impulses presented a much more difficult problem. These groups were especially dangerous to James if they arrived at conclusions radically different from his, yet maintained that these conclusions were products of similar methods.

[26] Henry James, *Christianity the Logic of Creation,* p. 76.
[27] Henry James, *The Nature of Evil,* p. 174.
[28] Henry James, *Society the Redeemed Form of Man,* p. 6.
[29] Henry James, *Substance and Shadow,* p. 199.
[30] Henry James, *Christianity the Logic of Creation,* p. 209.

The two communities with which James had the most contact were the Shakers and the Oneida Perfectionists. James dismissed the Shakers after a conversation with an elder of that church introduced to him by William Dean Howells. This old man had the temerity to suggest that Shakers led a life that was angelic. James seized upon this statement and countered vigorously with an opinion of his own to the effect that since angels were not conscious of their elevated position and only devils deceived themselves with angelic pretensions, the Shakers "were probably the sport of the hells."[31] Tolerating no angelic pretensions by anyone, James placed humility and a sense of sin high among the qualifications of a divine man. Then too, James objected to Shaker isolationism. Shakers preferred living in seclusion to living actively in society. To live the good life was to insulate oneself from society.

James wished to make an additional point against the religious disapprobation which descended upon the Oneida community, because that group had abandoned religious convention and had led disorderly lives, which failed to reflect the orderliness of creation. Perfectionist practices, under the aegis of John Humphrey Noyes, clearly fit James's definition of ideal action, since these practices were spontaneous with the individual. James saw the need to refute the implication that freedom of action would lead to disorderliness.[32] He asserted, as an article of faith, that free men behaved in a moral, orderly way.

By definition, no perfect institution could be found; however, the perfected *individual* was within the realm of possibility.[33] James searched his society for evidence of genius, symbolic of the man to be. One would logically assume that the realm in which these perfect individuals would be found was either in the creative arts or comparable intellectual activity.

The outstanding intellectual movement of James's day was Transcendentalism. Could an individual Transcendentalist be found who acted spontaneously, fulfilling physical and moral needs in the process, yet remaining humble and attributing his action to God, while maintaining an ideal fellowship with other men? James concluded that such a man could hardly be found among the Transcendentalists, who had made several basic ideological errors. One of the most common of these errors was the denial of the importance of education and the de-emphasis of past history, in

---

31 Howells, pp. 267-68.
32 Andrews, *Love, Marriage and Divorce,* p. 29.
33 Henry James, Jr., *Notes of a Son and Brother,* p. 233.

direct opposition to James's idea that historical change was one of the most important paths to the truth of man's ideal relation with his fellow man.

Another error of the Transcendentalists, however, loomed larger. James described the error in a letter to Edmund Tweedy, an old friend, while discussing the personality of Margaret Fuller. While Margaret Fuller had an excellent mind and splendid ambition, she was not a comfortable person to associate with, as she possessed an inordinate amount of self-esteem. Omnibus drivers and tailors made much more congenial companions,[34] since they lacked the overwhelming moral stuffiness of many of the Transcendentalists.

Emerson had the dubious honor of being the Transcendentalist with whom James had the closest contact. The many-sided Emerson proved an enigma to James. At times James was completely exasperated with him, comparing his ignorance to a child's failure to comprehend anything that was not immediately available through sense data.[35] How much Emerson's refusal to accept James's definition of reason and revelation had to do with this petulance is a matter of conjecture.

In addition, Emerson voiced several opinions with which James could not agree, since they seemed to limit man's freedom. James maintained that Emerson acted as if he believed that a life planned under divine aegis was superior to a free, unplanned one.[36] This misconception was minor, however, when compared to the major error of supposing that the morally better man had contributed more to society than the morally evil man. Moral distinctions were too absolute in Emerson's thought.[37]

Moral absolutism was the root of Emerson's trouble, James thought. Emerson was incapable of distinguishing between good and evil in himself; he could understand outward moral differences,[38] but he could not conceive that placing moral judgment was spiritual sin. Concerned as Emerson was over moral distinctions, he never possessed a sense of sin; or if he had one, it was so feeble that it did not compel him to search outside of himself for God. Emerson lived in innocence of spiritual sin.[39]

However, the incapacity for a sense of sin turned into an

[34] Perry, *The Thought and Character of William James*, p. 74.
[35] *Ibid.*, pp. 96-97.
[36] Henry James, *Society the Redeemed Form of Man*, p. 9.
[37] William James, p. 268.
[38] *Ibid.*, p. 297.
[39] Perry, p. 141.

advantage for Emerson, making an alert, independent mind possible.[40] Emerson, because of his innocence, was not afraid of tradition or of those who might oppose him, since he never doubted his ability and correctness. If he had even felt as helpless as James had, he would not have been so confident.

In his letter to Emerson in 1850, James indicated just how much the qualities of Emerson were worth to him. No one symbolized better how men would act in a perfect society than did Emerson. His rich, spontaneous public life provided a considerable contrast with the stunted private lives of men around him.[41] Emerson was important as he indicated how men would behave if given perfect freedom, although James did not agree that the intellectual conclusions reached by Emerson were necessarily valid. The spontaneous life of the Transcendentalists, best typified by Emerson, was their important contribution.

In evaluating foreign as well as domestic artists, James inevitably came into contact with English literature, which, like English economic institutions, was counted the best in the world. Among English writers, Dickens aroused James's ire because of his sentimental moralism. This moralism, according to James, was superficial and trite, concerned with emotional, physical needs. James maintained that Dickens' world was a plane surface, bounded on the four sides by the head, heart, stomach, and liver.[42] Dickens' simple opposition of virtue and vice, church and theater, displayed none of the subtle moral distinctions that pervaded his society; no man with healthy tastes enjoyed such an unreal dichotomy. The ideas of virtue in Dickens' novels were so naive that James concluded that if poverty, idiocy, and oppression vanished from the earth, Dickens would have had no virtues left and no plot for his novels. This proved to James how slavish and forced Dickens' talent was,[43] and how wrong an artist could be.

Thackeray fared somewhat better in James's hands. James, advertising the appearance of Thackeray before the New York Society of Merchants' Clerks, called him "the most thoughtful critic of manners and society, the subtlest humorist, and the most effective because the most genial satirist the age has known."[44] Thackeray uncovered more truth than Dickens did, because he

---

[40] *Ibid.,* p. 40.

[41] Henry James, "Emerson," *Atlantic Monthly,* XCIV (1904), 744.

[42] Perry, p. 137.

[43] Henry James, Review of *Vanity Fair or Becky Sharp, The Spirit of the Age,* I (1849), 50.

[44] Grattan, *The Three Jameses,* p. 62.

gently poked fun at institutions and created a more subtle set of moral distinctions. However, the qualities that distinguished Emerson reappeared in Thackeray, whose sense and experiences provided material for all that he wrote. "He is the merest boy," Emerson reported as James's comment on Thackeray,[45] not realizing that James had expressed the same opinion about him. The qualities of reflection and understanding, typical of a true adult, were conspicuous by their absence in Thackeray.

Critics of Trollope had maintained that he was ridiculous in suggesting, in one of his books, that a middle-aged woman was capable of being in love. James disagreed with this criticism and even supposed that Trollope had gone too far in anticipating this criticism, with the result that his characterization of this woman was passionless and bloodless.[46] James was certain that none of the authors of his day could contribute much to the body of existing knowledge about human nature; but he had not expected them to diminish it, as Trollope had done.[47] By deliberately discounting man's physical and emotional needs, Trollope had created a false impression of human nature.

These three English novelists, Dickens, Thackeray and Trollope, all received rather harsh treatment in James's hands, for James's criticism of literature consisted almost entirely of an evaluation of content, with very little emphasis upon form or style. In order to satisfy James the content had to approximate his own ideas. Thus, Thackeray failed to draw the proper conclusions from a correct picture of society; Dickens estimated morality in a singularly gross fashion; and Trollope erred in analyzing human nature. The conclusion James reached seemed to be that the important English men of letters were simple, unimaginative fellows, highly susceptible to error; or if free from error, incapable of drawing proper conclusions from correct sources.

The giant in English letters, according to James, was not a novelist but rather the essayist and historian, Thomas Carlyle. James even declared to Emerson that Carlyle was the writer of greatest importance for the day because of his assimilation of the reality of evil. However, James later amended his opinion of Carlyle, for there were serious flaws in Carlyle's thought. One of these was Carlyle's excessive delicacy and aristocratic taste, as this story might indicate:

---

[45] Edward Waldo Emerson, *The Early Years of the Saturday Club*, p. 324.
[46] Henry James, Review of Trollope's *Miss Mackenzie*, *The Nation*, I (1865), 51.
[47] *Ibid.*, p. 52.

Twenty years after, the elder Henry James was saying in Boston that Carlyle had been vexed at Alcott's refusal to eat what was set before him at breakfast. He had sent out for some strawberries for the vegetarian's special benefit, and when these were put on the table Alcott was said to have taken them on the same plate with his potatoes, so that "the two juices ran together and fraternized." Carlyle was almost made ill apparently, by this revolting spectacle, so that he could eat nothing himself "but stormed up and down the room instead."[48]

Carlyle's main intellectual fault was similar to Emerson's. Carlyle had the advantage insofar as he indicated the reality of evil in the world, while Emerson hesitated to admit even its probable existence. Carlyle, however, emphasized the struggle between good and evil, making this struggle even more real by attributing strength to evil. Having done this, Carlyle went no further, a major error, since James wanted him to dismiss the moral struggle as temporary.[49]

Since the moral struggle in process the world over was the most important aspect of society, Carlyle was forced to glorify the characteristics that enabled man to win in this battle. Even men like Danton and Mirabeau, who were vagabonds in James's eyes, received special treatment from Carlyle because of their force of will.[50] The possibility of finding virtue in will was alien to James's thought, for he considered will to be the agent of sin. James and Carlyle had radically different opinions about the worth of one of the most conspicuous human qualities.

As moral force was the primary consideration for Carlyle, he could only sympathize with those who lacked this essential virtue and could not feel any common bond with them. Toward his friends he felt merely compassion rather than love. Men with whom he did feel a bond were Mohamet, William the Conqueror, Frederick II of Prussia, and Goethe — men who had proved their superior will by their worldly success. James maintained that Carlyle made another error in assuming that everyone who deserved to be successful was successful.[51]

Besides his mistaken evaluation of man's qualities, Carlyle made another mistake about the nature of society. Society was, for Carlyle, only "an empirical necessity of the race," contrary to James's

---

[48] Odell Shepard, *Pedlar's Progress*, p. 317.

[49] Perry, *The Thought and Character of William James*, pp. 141-42.

[50] Henry James, "Some Personal Recollections of Carlyle," *Atlantic Monthly*, XLVII (1881), 596.

[51] Edward Waldo Emerson, *Early Years of the Saturday Club*, p. 330.

definition of society as a necessary "organic unity." Assuming that
the institutions of society were artificial, Carlyle concluded that
the spirit of society was artificial also, functioning only as man
needed it.[52] While James recognized the artificiality of existing
institutions, he insisted that the spirit of society was inherent in
man. Starting as he had from the unequal characteristics of man,
Carlyle inevitably reached his conclusion about the nature of
society. Had he been less interested in heroes and more in the
common man, this mistaken concept of society would never
have occurred. James scored Carlyle repeatedly for his hero worship and compared him with the reformers whom James had also
attacked.[53]

Originally, Carlyle had possessed a talent for making a complete, unified picture out of the bits and shreds of historical evidence, but James considered that the imaginative faculty was
leaving him and was being replaced by hackneyed habit.[54] This,
in the final analysis, indicated Carlyle's symbolic worth. Carlyle
represented the age in which he lived far better than anyone else,
carrying the emphasis upon morality to its logical conclusion. He
was able to do this, according to James, because he was a Scotch-
man, with Calvinist foundations, influenced by German romanticism.[55] If Emerson represented the new, spiritual man, Carlyle
surely epitomized the old, moral one.

That James's tastes in literature, as in life, ran toward tragedy is
illustrated by some comments contained in a letter which he wrote
to Turgenev, one of the few non-English or non-American literary
men that James liked. Other literary critics had called Turgenev
a cynic for portraying man struggling in vain to escape the bonds
of social and physical nature. Pleased with an assumption so similar to his own, James assigned great merit to Turgenev's works,
which gave men valuable insights into the hearts and minds of
other men. James believed, as we have seen, that education and
knowledge turned into love and brotherhood, so that Turgenev
was furthering the spirit of fellowship.[56] Perhaps contemporary
literature could show no finer example of artistic merit than Turgenev's tragic hero.

Two other men struck James as possessing a large amount of

---

[52] Henry James, Review of Carlyle's *Frederick the Great, The Nation,* I
(1865), 21.
[53] Warren, *The Elder Henry James,* p. 54.
[54] Henry James, Review of *Frederick the Great,* p. 21.
[55] Perry, *The Thought and Character of William James,* p. 47.
[56] *Ibid.,* pp. 138-39.

spontaneous, artistic life. These men were Oliver Wendell Holmes and John Stuart Mill. For sheer intellectual energy, the prize went to Dr. Holmes. Holmes, said James, was the most intellectually alive man he had ever known. Mill's ideas, as propounded in his book on liberty, reflected a man whose primary concern was to sympathize with and enlighten human nature.[57] The intellectual abilities of Mill were tempered by an emotional bias toward human qualities, a combination which James greatly admired. Lacking only the background of a more flexible early training, Mill approached closer to the artistic ideal of James than anyone else.

Perhaps a composite individual could be plotted who would combine all the necessary elements and would present the prototype of the perfect individual. This ideal individual would have a sense of sin comparable to Carlyle's combined with Turgenev's tragic sense of life. Physical needs would not be discounted by this individual as by Thackeray, and he would possess the self-assurance and spontaneity of Emerson. Holmes could contribute his quick, active mind to be amalgamated in the tempered union of reason and emotion in Mill. This, then, would be man as he would exist in a redeemed society — not that this man contained any new virtues, virtues uncommon to James's society, but that he combined many old virtues. James did not, however, suppose that all individuals in the perfect society would be the same; rather he expected diversity.

In looking over contemporary men and society James found support for some of his views. He concluded that American society in all its phases, social, political, economic, and religious, was the most advanced in the world. This conclusion was proved by the advanced institutional disorganization in the United States. Conversely, the education of American citizens had progressed so that Americans were the most individualistic and yet the most socially minded of all people. In America, institutional decay and individual social education went hand in hand.

The discovery of a genius who combined spontaneous activity with a sensitive social conscience proved more difficult for James than finding evidence of a dying social order. James nowhere succeeded in finding a perfect man, although he found many of the virtues of a perfect man. Perhaps, in the final analysis, a perfect individual would not be found until a perfect society existed.

---

[57] Warren, *The Elder Henry James,* p. 52.

Conclusion

Political democracy, as it exists and practically works in America, with all its threatening evils, supplies a training school for making first-class men. It is life's gymnasium, not of good only, but of all. . . . Not for nothing does evil play its part among us. Judging from the main portions of the history of the world, so far, justice is always in jeopardy, peace walks amid hourly pitfalls, and of slavery, misery, meanness, the craft of tyrants and the credulity of the populace, in some of their protean forms, no voice can at any time say, They are not.[1]

Many similar observations might be found in almost any of James's books and articles, for James never assumed that the truth would be hurt by repetition; yet this particular selection came, not from James, but from the nineteenth-century democratic poet Walt Whitman, noted more for his earlier, ecstatic celebration of life than as the later essayist concerned with the problem of evil.

The reason for including a portion from Whitman's *Democratic Vistas* is not to intimate that there was any close connection between Whitman and James, but rather to point out some common assumptions. Whitman shared with James a belief in the educative function of evil, although he assigned a different reason for the existence of evil. In his own way, conversely, James assumed some of the tenets of the mid-nineteenth-century romantic American thinkers, epitomized by Whitman's almost religious conception of American democracy.

James partook of the liberal tradition. Believing as he did in man's absolute freedom, he assumed that this freedom could result in injury to no one. One can hardly imagine a belief more optimistic than his belief in a harmonious universe. James's ideas were, perhaps, liberal ideas carried as far as possible into an idealized anarchism.

This social and political anarchism came to James through re-

---

[1] Walt Whitman, *Democratic Vistas* (New York: E. P. Dutton, 1912), p. 322.

ligious suppositions that were more conservative than the liberal theologies of the day, Unitarianism and Transcendentalism. James emphasized evil in reaction against these movements that had concentrated upon man's better nature. James insisted upon the absolute power and sovereignty of God as well as on the necessity of Christ (with some modifications).

However, the necessity of individual salvation, a point of great concern for the Calvinist, was a matter of little interest to James, for he was intrigued with the possibility of combining evil and good to form a new, perfect society. Although James started with Calvinistic ideas and used Calvinistic terminology, he reached conclusions which were far more similar to those of the Unitarians and Transcendentalists. His use of traditional religious thought also resulted in political and social ideas similar to those held by many Americans of his age. At the base of his thought we can locate Ralph Henry Gabriel's definition of the tenets of American faith. Gabriel holds that four elements composed America's democratic ideology: a faith in the free individual, a belief in an all-persuasive moral law, a goal of Manifest Destiny for the United States, and a hope for unceasing progress on all levels.

The latter two ideas were connected for James, as they were for most American thinkers. James maintained as an article of faith, that society would progress to perfection; he held to this more strongly than to anything else. Feeling life not worth living without a faith in progress, James made his hope of God contingent upon this. Progress was shown best in America whose destiny was to demonstrate the advantages of freedom to the world. The end for James was the same as for any expansionist who excused the acquisition of Mexico and Oregon with the maxim of the superiority of American democracy.

The contradiction which Gabriel found between his concept of the free individual and his concept of obedience to a higher moral law did not exist for James. His faith in the essential goodness of human nature, when allowed to have free play, led him to believe that no moral law was necessary, since spontaneous action, by definition, could not be immoral. The moral law could be dispensed with in favor of a spirit of fellowship, which this law helped to engender. No limit should be placed on man's freedom; this was James's primary concern.

James's social and political ideals expressed a peculiar nineteenth-century American belief in the free individual's ability to live harmoniously in a society free from compulsion. James, therefore, had more in common with the thinkers of his age than either he or they suspected, since, in spite of their opinions of each other, for all their assumption of different roads, the result was the same — an American faith.

Bibliography

I. Works by James

A. Books

James, Henry. *Christianity the Logic of Creation.* New York: D. Appleton and Company, 1857.
————. *The Church of Christ Not an Ecclesiasticism.* 2nd ed., London: Walton and Mitchell, 1856.
————. *Lectures and Miscellanies.* New York: Redfield, 1852.
Sandeman, Robert. *Letters on Theron and Aspasio.* Edited and prefaced by Henry James. New York: John S. Taylor, 1838.
The Literary Remains of Henry James, ed. William James. Cambridge: University Press, 1884.
Hennequin, Victor. *Love in a Phalastery.* Translated and prefaced by Henry James. New York: Dewett and Davenport, 1848.
James, Henry, Stephen Pearl Andrews and Horace Greeley. *Love, Marriage and Divorce and the Sovereignty of the Individual.* New York: Stringer and Townsend, 1853.
James, Henry. *Moralism and Christianity.* New York: Redfield, 1850.
————. *The Nature of Evil.* New York: D. Appleton and Co., 1855.
————. *Remarks on the Apostolic Gospel.* 1840 Extant.
————. *The Secret of Swedenborg.* Boston: Fields, Osgood and Company, 1869.
————. *The Social Significance of Our Institutions.* Boston: Tichnor and Fields, 1861.
————. *Society the Redeemed Form of Man.* Boston: Houghton, Osgood and Company, 1879.
————. *Substance and Shadow.* Boston: Tichnor and Fields, 1863.
————. *Tracts for the New Times. No. I, Letter to a Swedenborgian.* New York: John Allen, 1847.
————. *What Constitutes the State?* New York: John Allen, 1846.

B. Articles and Letters

————. "The Bible in the Public Schools," *Atlantic Monthly,* XXV (1870), 638.
————. "Emerson," *Atlantic Monthly,* XCIV (1904), 740-45.
————. "Emmanuel Swedenborg," *Nation,* IV (1866), 329.
————. "Faith and Science," *North American Review,* CI (1865), 335-78.
————. "The Logic of Marriage and Murder," *Atlantic Monthly,* XXV (1870), 744-49.
————. "The Radical Dogmatics," *The Radical,* II (1867), 84-94.

————. "A Scientific Statement of the Lord of Divine Man," *Massachusetts Quarterly Review*, III (1850), 52-67.

————. "Some Personal Recollections of Carlyle," *Atlantic Monthly*, XLVII (1881), 593-609.

————. "Spiritualism New and Old," *Atlantic Monthly*, XXIX (1872), 358-72.

————. "Stephen Dewhurst's *Autobiography*," *Atlantic Monthly*, LIV (1884), 649-62.

————. "Swedenborg as a Theologian," *Massachusetts Quarterly Review*, I (1848), 293-307.

————. "Swedenborg's Ontology," *North American Review*, CV (1867), 89-193.

————. "Woman and the Woman's Movement," *Putnam's Monthly Magazine*, I (1853), 279-88.

————. "The Woman Thou Gavest Me," *Atlantic Monthly*, XXV (1870), 66-72.

————. Letter to Francis Ellingwood Abbot, "Deliverance, not Perfection, The Aim of Religion," *The Index*, VII (1867), 26.

————. Letter to F.E.A., "The Reconciliation of Man Individual with Man Universal," *The Index*, VII (1867), 52.

————. Letter to F.E.A., "Society versus Selfhood," *The Index*, VII (1876), 74-75.

————. Letter to F.E.A., "Spiritual Creation," *The Index*, VII (1876), 134-35.

————. Letter to F.E.A., "Knowledge and Science Contrasted," *The Index*, VII (1876), 172-73.

————. Letter to F.E.A., "The Philosophy of the Heart," *The Index*, VII (1876), 230-31.

————. Review of B. F. Barrett's *The Golden City*, *Atlantic Monthly*, XXXIII (1874), 236.

————. Review of Henry Ward Beecher's *Lecture Room Talks*, *Atlantic Monthly*, XXVI (1870), 118-19.

————. Review of William Blake's *Poems*, *The Spirit of the Age*, I (1849), 113.

————. Review of Horace Bushnell's *Vicarious Sacrifice*, *North American Review*, CII (1866), 556-571.

————. Review of Thomas Carlyle's *Frederick the Great*, *The Nation*, I (1865), 20-21.

————. Review of the Cincinnati Superior Court's Decision, "The Bible in the Public Schools," *Atlantic Monthly*, XXV (1870), 638.

————. Review of Rufus W. Clark's *The Question of the Hour*, *Atlantic Monthly*, XXV (1870), 638-39.

————. Review of F. P. Coble's *Religious Duty*, *The Nation*, I (1865), 249-50.

————. Review of D. Norman Foster's translation of *The True Christian Religion*, *Atlantic Monthly*, XXIII (1869), 765-67.

————. Review of William Hamilton's *Works*, *Putnam's Monthly Magazine*, II (1853), 470-81.

————. Review of Henry C. Lee's *A History of Sacerdotal Celibacy in the Christian Church*, *Atlantic Monthly*, XX (1867), 378-83.

————. Review of H. F. Lecky's *History of the Rise and Influence of the*

Spirit of Rationalism in Europe, Atlantic Monthly, XVII (1866), 248-51.

————. Review of James Legge's *The Chinese Classics, Atlantic Monthly,* XXV (1870), 763-64.

————. Review of Nietzsche's *Ecce Homo, Atlantic Monthly,* XVII (1866), 122-23.

————. Review of J. C. Shairp's *Culture and Religion in Some of Their Relations, Atlantic Monthly,* XXVIII (1871), 252-54.

————. Review of Stirling's *Secret of Hegel, North American Review,* CII (1866), 264-75.

————. Review of *Vanity Fair or Becky Sharp, The Spirit of the Age,* I (1849), 49-50.

————. Review of Alfred Russel Wallace's *Contributions to the Theory of Natural Selection, Atlantic Monthly,* XXVI (1870), 757-59.

————. Review of M. J. Williamson's *Modern Diabolism, Atlantic Monthly,* XXXII (1873), 219-24.

II. Relevant to the Study of James

A. Books

Alcott, A. Bronson. *Concord Days.* Boston: Roberts Brothers, 1888.

Barrett, Benjamin F. *The Golden Reed.* New York: D. Appleton and Co., 1855.

Beach, Joseph Warren. *The Method of Henry James.* New York: Yale University Press, 1918.

Blau, Joseph L., ed. *American Philosophic Addresses, 1700-1900.* New York: Columbia University Press, 1946.

Boxler, Julius Seelye. *Religion in the Philosophy of William James.* Boston: Marshall Jones Company, 1926.

Block, Marguerite Beck. *The New Church in the New World.* New York: Henry Holt and Co., 1932.

Boaz, George. *Romanticism in America.* Baltimore: John Hopkins Press, 1940.

Brooks, Van Wyck. *The Flowering of New England.* New York: E. P. Dutton and Company, 1940.

————. *New England: Indian Summer.* New York: E. P. Dutton and Company, 1940.

————. *The Pilgrimage of Henry James.* New York: E. P. Dutton and Company, 1925.

————. *The Times of Melville and Whitman.* New York: E. P. Dutton and Company, 1947.

Brownson, Orestes A. *Essays and Reviews.* New York: P. J. Kenedy and Sons, n.d.

Cameron, Kenneth Walter. *Emerson the Essayist,* vol. II. Raleigh, North Carolina: The Thistle Press, 1945.

Cantwell, Robert. *Nathaniel Hawthorne: The American Years.* New York: Rinehart and Company, 1948.

Carlyle, Thomas. *The Correspondence of Thomas Carlyle and Ralph Waldo Emerson,* vols. I and II. Boston: Tichnor and Company, 1888.

Channing, William Ellery. *Discourses, Reviews and Miscellanies.* Boston: Hendee and Company, 1830.

————. *Works.* Boston: American Unitarian Association, 1899.
Codman, John Thomas. *Brook Farm.* Boston: Arena Publishing Company, 1894.
Cooke, George Willis. *Unitarianism in America.* Boston: American Unitarian Association, 1910.
Ekrich, Arthur A. *The Idea of Progress in America, 1815-1860.* New York: Columbia University Press, 1944.
Emerson, Edward Waldo. *The Early Years of the Saturday Club.* Boston: Houghton Mifflin Company, 1918.
Emerson, Ralph Waldo. *Nature.* Edited with introduction by Kenneth Walter Cameron. New York: Scholars' fácsimiles and reprints, 1940.
————. *Representative Men.* Boston: Houghton Mifflin Company, 1876.
Gabriel, Ralph Henry. *The Course of American Democratic Thought.* New York: The Ronald Press, 1940.
Goddard, Harold Clarke. *Studies in New England Transcendentalism.* New York: Columbia University Press, 1908.
Grattan, Clinton Hartley. *The Three Jameses.* New York: Longmans, Green and Company, 1932.
Hall, T. C. *The Religious Background of American Culture.* Boston: Little, Brown and Company, 1930.
Haroutunian, Joseph. *Piety versus Moralism.* New York: Henry Holt and Company, 1932.
Howe, Julia Ward. *Reminiscences.* Boston: Houghton Mifflin and Company, 1900.
Howe, Mark Antony De Wolfe. *The Later Years of the Saturday Club.* Boston: Houghton Mifflin and Company, 1900.
Howells, William Dean. *Literary Friends and Acquaintances.* New York: Harper and Brothers, 1900.
James, Alice. *Alice James: Her Brothers, Her Journals,* ed. Anna Robeson Burr. New York: Dodd, Mead and Company, 1934.
James, Henry, Jr. *The Letters of Henry James,* ed. Percy Lubbock. New York: Charles Scribner's Sons, 1920.
————. *Notes of a Son and Brother.* New York: Charles Scribner's Sons, 1914.
————. *A Small Boy and Others.* New York: Charles Scribner's Sons, 1913.
James, Henry, III. *The Letters of William James.* Boston: The Atlantic Monthly Press, 1920.
Lewis, R. W. B. *The American Adam.* Chicago: The University of Chicago Press, 1955.
Macintosh, Douglas Clyde. *The Problem of Religious Knowledge.* New York: Harper and Brothers, 1940.
Matthiessen, F. O. *American Renaissance.* New York: Oxford University Press, 1941.
————. *The James Family.* New York: Alfred A. Knopf, 1947.
Marx, Leo. *The Machine in the Garden.* New York: Oxford University Press, 1964.
Miller, Perry. *The Transcendentalists.* Cambridge: Harvard University Press, 1950.
Mumford, Lewis. *The Golden Day.* New York: Boni and Liveright, 1926.
Odhner, Carl Theophilis. *Annals of the New Church, 1688-1850,* vol. I. Bryn-Athyn, Penna.: Academy of the New Church, 1904.
Ossoli, Margaret Fuller. *Art, Literature and the Drama,* ed. Arthur B. Fuller. Boston: Robert Brothers, 1875.

Pattee, Fred Lewis. *The Feminine Fifties.* New York: D. Appleton-Century Company, 1940.

Patterson, Robert Leet. *The Philosophy of William Ellery Channing.* New York: Bookman Associates, 1952.

Perry, Ralph Barton. *Puritanism and Democracy.* New York: Vanguard Press, 1944.

——. *The Thought and Character of William James,* vols. I and III. Boston: Little, Brown and Company, 1935.

Persons, Stow. *Free Religion.* New Haven: Yale University Press, 1947.

Pockmann, Henry A. *New England Transcendentalism and St. Louis Hegelianism.* Philadelphia: Carl Shurz, Memorial Foundation, Inc., 1948.

Riley, Woodbridge. *American Thought from Puritanism to Pragmatism and Beyond.* New York: Henry Holt and Company, 1915.

Rogers, A. K. *Morals on Review.* New York: The Macmillan Company, 1927.

Rollo, Ogden, ed. *Life and Letters of Edwin Lawrence Godkin,* vols. I and II. New York: The Macmillan Company, 1902.

Sargent, Mrs. John T. *Sketches and Reminiscences of the Radical Club.* Boston: James R. Osgood and Company, 1880.

Sears, Clara Endicott. *Bronson Alcott's Fruitlands.* Boston: Houghton Mifflin Company, 1915.

Schlesinger, Arthur M., Jr. *Orestes A. Brownson: A Pilgrim's Progress.* Boston: Little, Brown and Company, 1939.

Schneider, Herbert W. *A History of American Philosophy.* New York: Columbia University Press, 1946.

Schneider, Herbert W., and George Lawton. *A Prophet and a Pilgrim.* New York: Columbia University Press, 1942.

Seldes, Gilbert. *The Stammering Century.* New York: The John Day Company, 1927.

Shepard, Odell, ed. *Journals of Bronson Alcott.* Boston: Little, Brown and Company, 1938.

——. *Pedlar's Progress.* Boston: Little, Brown, and Company, 1937.

Silver, Ednah C. *Sketches of the New Church in America.* Boston: The Massachusetts New Church Union, 1920.

Swedenborg, Emmanuel. *Conjugal Love.* New York: American Swedenborg Printing and Publishing Society, 1892.

——. *Heaven and Hell.* New York: Swedenborg Foundation, Inc., 1946.

——. *The True Christian Religion.* New York: American Swedenborg Printing and Publishing Society, 1898.

Toksvig, Signe. *Emmanuel Swedenborg.* New Haven: Yale University Press, 1948.

Townsend, Harvey Gates. *Philosophical Ideas in the United States.* New York: American Book Company, Inc., 1944.

Trowbridge, George. *Swedenborg, Life and Teaching.* New York: Swedenborg Foundation, Inc., 1920.

Tyler, Alice Felt. *Freedom's Ferment.* Minneapolis: University of Minnesota Press, 1944.

Warren, Austin. *The Elder Henry James.* New York: The Macmillan Company, 1934.

Wells, Ronald Vale. *Three Christian Transcendentalists.* New York: Columbia University Press, 1943.

Whitman, Walt. *Leaves of Grass and Democratic Vistas.* New York: E. P. Dutton and Company, 1912.

Wieman, Henry Nelson and Bernard Eugene Meland. *American Philosophies of Religion*. New York: Willett, Clark and Company, 1936.
Wilkinson, J. J. Garth. *The African and the True Christian Church*. London: The New-Church Press, Ltd., 1892.
Young, Frederick Harold. *The Philosophy of Henry James, Sr.* New York: Bookman Associates, 1951.

B. Articles

Abbot, Francis Ellingwood. Editorial reply to James, *The Index*, VII (1876), 30-31.
———. Editorial reply to James, *The Index*, VII (1876), 54.
———. Editorial reply to James, *The Index*, VII (1876), 78-79.
———. Editorial reply to James, *The Index*, VII (1876), 138.
———. Editorial reply to James, *The Index*, VII (1876), 174-75.
Albee, John. Review of William James's *Literary Remains of Henry James, Journal of Speculative Philosophy*, XIX (1885), 435-37.
Anderson, Quentin. "Henry James and the New Jerusalem," *Kenyon Review*, VIII (1946), 515-28, 532-34, 536, 538, 540-42, 565.
———. "The Two Henry James," *Scrutiny*, XIV (1947), 242-251.
Baugh, Hansell, "Emerson and the Elder Henry James," *The Bookman*, LXVIII (1928), 320-22.
Clarke, James Freeman. Review of Henry James's *The Nature of Evil, Christian Examiner*, LIX (1855), 116-136.
———. Review of Henry James's *Substance and Shadow, Christian Examiner*, LXXV (1863), 212-224.
Galbraith, W. H. Review of Henry James's *Society the Redeemed Form of Man, New Church Independent*, XXVII (1879), 229-235.
Howells, William. Review of Henry James's *The Secret of Swedenborg, The Atlantic Monthly*, XXIV (1869), 762-63.
———. "Some Literary Memories of Cambridge," Part II, *Harper's Magazine*, CL (1900), 828-831.
Howison, George H. Review of Henry James's *Society the Redeemed Form of Man, Christian Register*, LVIII (1879).
Kimball, W. H. "Swedenborg and Henry James," *Journal of Speculative Philosophy*, XVII (1883), 113-130.
Lackland, C. E. "Henry James the Seer," *Journal of Speculative Philosophy*, (1885), 53-60.
Larabee, Harold A. "The James: Financier, Heretic and Philosopher," *The American Scholar*, I (1932), 401-413.
———. "Flight of Henry James the First," *New England Quarterly*, X (1937), 774-75.
Markham, Edwin. "Distinguished American Family," *Cosmopolitan*, L (1910), 145-46.
Mulford, E. Review of William James's *The Literary Remains of Henry James, The Atlantic Monthly*, LV (1885), 702-05.
Orr, A. Review of Henry James's *Society the Redeemed Form of Man*. No. 2752 (1880), 113-15.
Perry, Ralph Barton. "Religion versus Morality according to the Elder Henry James," *International Journal of Ethics*, XLII (1932), 283-303.
Pierce, Charles Saunders. Review of *The Secret of Swedenborg, North American Review*, CX (1870), 463-68.

Sears, E. H. Review of Henry James's *Substance and Shadow, Atlantic Monthly,* LV (1885).

Sechrist, Alice Spiers. *Tribute to Henry James, Sr., Atlantic Monthly,* LV (1885), 706-08.

Warren, Austin. "James and His Secret," *Saturday Review of Literature,* VIII (1932), 759.

Index

Academy Movement 41, 42
Adam 58
Alcott, A. Bronson 22, 26, 27, 30, 32, 135
American Enlightenment 9
Anarchism, ideal 138
Andrews, Stephen Pearl 105
Anti-institutionalism 11
Antinomianism 14, 73, 96
Anti-slavery Movement 123
Apostle John 119
Apostolic Gospel 9
Appomattox 10
Arcana Caelestia 44
Art 93, 94
Atheism 73

Beecher, Rev. Lyman 128
Bird, Rev. William 35
Boadicea 75
"Boston principle" 39
Boyle, Rev. 35
Brook Farm 23, 30
Brooks, Van Wyck 124
Brownson, Orestes 21, 29
Buchanan, James 125
Buckminister, Rev. Joseph 16
Bushnell, Dr. Horace 128

Calvinism 13, 16, 20, 21, 22, 24, 130
Carlyle, Thomas 32, 134, 135, 136
  Definition of society 135
Catherine of Russia 75
Channing, Edward 17, 19, 20, 22
Choice 130
Christ 66, 67, 72
Christian Education 5
Christianity 18, 30
Christian Sciences 5

Church 110
  Membership 35
Circumcision 15
Civilization, definition 106
Civil War 9, 125
Classes
  Priests 91
  Soldiers 91
  Merchants and commercial men 91
Collectivism 11
Colonies 13
Commune form 115
Comte 48
Confession 88
Congregationalists 22
Conjugal-heresy 39
Conscience, definition 87
Conservatives 22
The Convert 21
Cosmology 19
Council of Menes 44
Cox, Harvey 5
Creation 51, 53
  Spiritual 54
Crime 121
Crusades 9

Danton, George Jacques 135
Davis, Jefferson 125
Declaration of Independence 84, 127
Deism 31, 109
Democracy 120
Democratic Vistas 138
Depravity 18
Dewhurst, Stephen 63
Dickens, Charles 133
Divine-Natural-Humanity 45, 63

Divorce 116
Doctrine of depravity 22
Doctrine of Trinity 18
Dualism 73

1820's 17
1860's 10
1870's 10
Eddy, Mary Baker 37
Education 21, 64
Emerson, Edward Waldo 10, 22, 24, 32, 33, 64, 132-136
Evangelical systems 24
Eve 58
Everett, Alexander H. 22
Evil 14, 49, 67
    Institutionalized 29
    Moral 59, 61
    Physical 59, 61
    Spiritual 59
Evolution 101, 102
    Naturalism 11

Faith 17
Family 117
    Definition 29
Fourier 41, 127
Franklin, Benjamin 27
Frederick II of Prussia 135
Freedom 18, 20, 21, 54, 55, 92
    Absolute 138
    Moral 34
Freudians 93
Fuller, Margaret 22, 33, 132

Gabriel, Ralph Henry 139
Genius 92, 108
God 17
Godkin, E. L. 75
Goethe 135
Government 20, 21, 119
Grace 18
Grattan, Clinton Hartley 124
Greeley, Horace 116
The Growth of the Mind 25

Habit 93
Haeckle, Ernst 101
Harmony 93
Hawthorne, Nathaniel 10
Heaven 62
Hebrew 15

Hegelian 73, 91
Hell 62
History 65
    Definition 98, 99
Holmes, Oliver Wendell 137
Homeopathy 41
Hopkins, Samuel 15
Howe, Julia Ward 55
Howells, William Dean 45, 131
Humanitarian movements 10
Human race 74
Humility 91
Huxley, Thomas Henry 101

Idealism 22, 73, 139
Independence 56
Individual 21, 91
    Perfect 137
    Radical 11
Inferiority 75
Insecurity 52
Instinctual stage 77
Institutions 5
    Scottish 25

Jackson, Gen. 119
James, Henry 5
James, Henry, Sr. 31
    Definition of society 136
    Difference from Swedenborg 47
    Definition of religion 47
    Spheres, real and unreal 71
James, William 66
Jesus, concept of 72
Justice 20

Kant, Immanuel 22
Knowledge 64
Kramer, Christian 36

Laws
    Marriage 120
    Secular 121
Liberties
    Civil 18
    Political 18
Liberty 18
Life
    After death 36
    Mental 77
    Physical 77
    Stages 77

Lincoln, Abraham 125
Lockean 25
  Sensate Psychology 24
Love 14, 17

Man
  Action 78
  Freedom 78
  Spiritual 90
  vs. woman 75
Manichean 128
Manifest Destiny 139
Marriage
  In heaven 34, 36
  Laws 120
  Socialization 116
Marsh, James 24, 25
Marx, Leo 11, 127
Materialist 91
Matriarchy 76
Mayhew, Jonathan 18
Mazzini, Giuseppe 119
Melville, Herman 10
Methodism 5
Microcosm 23
Mill, John Stuart 75, 137
Mind 57
Mirabeau, Honore Gabriel Victor
  Riqueti 135
Miracles 19, 65, 66
Missouri Compromise 10
Mohamet 135
Monism 23, 73
Moral 20, 21
  Judgments 18
  Law 64, 85
  Pride 86
Morality 15, 20
Mormonism 130
Murder 85

Napoleon, Louis 119
Naturalists 26
Nature 20, 56, 57
  Definition 27
New England 16, 25
  Theology 16
New Jerusalem Magazine 129
The North American Review 22
Norton, Andrews 28
Noyes, John Humphrey 131

Obedience 19
Old Theology 51
Oneida Perfectionists 131
Osgood, Samuel 27

Paganism 70
Pain 81
Pantheism 73, 91
Parker, Theodore 22, 24, 31
Peabody, Elizabeth 30
Perfectibility 11
Perfection 50, 131, 137
Perry, John 36
Perry, Ralph Barton 83, 108
Phelps, Francis 36
Phrenology 41
Physical
  Needs 80
  Sin 80
Piety 21
Power 26
Pride 64
Progress 30, 122, 123
  Moral 30
Property 118
Proselytes 35
Protestantism 21, 113, 114
Proudhon, Pierre Joseph 128
Puritan 16, 19, 22

Quakerism 22
Queen Elizabeth 75
Queen Ulrica Eleanor 44

Rationalism 21
Reason 19, 25
  Definition 98
  Deductive 26
  Inductive 26
Rebaptism 40
Redemption 63
Reed, Sampson 25, 36
Regeneration 18, 58
  Natural 68
  Spiritual 68
Religion 21, 23, 25
  Natural 109
  Philosophical 23
Republicans 9, 125
Revelation 19, 66
Reverence 19
Revivalism 111

Revolt 36
Righteousness 18
Ripley, George 23, 30
Ritualism 110, 111
Roche, Rev. Manning B. 35
Roe, Daniel 39
Roman Catholic Church 113
Romantic 5, 21

Sabbatarians 43
Salvation 15, 18, 61, 62, 63, 66, 68
Sandeman, Robert 43
Sandemanians 44
Science
  Definition 99, 100
  Universal 101
Sectarian 114
Self
  External 79
  Internal 79
  Self-righteousness 61, 86
  Selfhood 60, 66
  Self-reliant 56
Shakers 131
Sin 14, 19, 20, 49
Slavery 9, 108, 125
Social
  Change 9
  Displacement 10
  Forms 115
  Life 64
  Ties 108
Socialist 122
  Utopian 127
Socialization 24
Society 5, 105, 108
  Carlyle's definition 135
  Cincinnati 39
  Definition 29
  James's definition 136
  Voluntary 123
Soul 21, 23
Spontaneous 93, 96
  Stage 77
States rights 9
Sterling, John 91
Steven, Rev. Joseph 16

Swedenborg, Emmanuel 22, 25, 32,
  33, 44, 45, 64, 128, 129
Symbolism 23
  Natural 65

Temperance cause 123
Temple School 27, 30
Territorial expansion 9
Thackeray, William 133, 134
Thoreau, Henry David 10, 105,
  107
Time lag 106
Transcendentalist 13, 19, 22, 23,
  131
  Christian 24
  Institutional 11
  Laws of nature 26
  Religion 31
Trollope, Anthony 134
Truth 18, 23
Turgenev, Ivan 136
Tweedy, Edmund 132

Understanding 25
Unitarianism 13, 16, 18, 20, 21,
  22, 130
Unity 95
Universalists 16, 130
Universe 15, 19
Unreal 71
Upsala University 44
Utilitarians 24
Utopian 5
  Socialist 127

Vice 121
Voluntary stage 77

Webster, Noah 27
Weeks, Rev. Holland 35
Whigs 9
Whitman, Walt 10, 138
Wilkinson, J. J. Garth 45
William the Conqueror 135
Woman 75, 76
Worship 21

Young, Frederick 46